D0069804

GANDHI

Pietermaritzburg railway station, South Africa, winter, 1893. In the station waiting room, which is dark and bitterly cold, a well dressed young Indian man is sitting. In his pocket there is a first class ticket from Durban to Pretoria, but he has only done part of the journey. A few hours earlier, the guard had asked police to take him off the train. A white passenger wanted to ride in the first class compartment – but not while an Indian man was there. To the railway company and the police, this was quite normal.

But not to Mohandas Gandhi. As the night goes on, he wonders what to do. Should he keep quiet? Should he go back to India? Or should he fight against this injustice? By morning, Gandhi has decided to fight – and he has taken a first step on the path that will one day make him a leader loved and followed by millions, even years after his death.

OXFORD BOOKWORMS LIBRARY
Factfiles

Gandhi

Stage 4 (1400 headwords)

Factfiles Series Editor: Christine Lindop

ROWENA AKINYEMI

Gandhi

OXFORD UNIVERSITY PRESS

OXFORD
UNIVERSITY PRESS

Great Clarendon Street, Oxford OX2 6DP

Oxford University Press is a department of the University of Oxford.
It furthers the University's objective of excellence in research, scholarship,
and education by publishing worldwide in

Oxford New York

Auckland Cape Town Dar es Salaam Hong Kong Karachi
Kuala Lumpur Madrid Melbourne Mexico City Nairobi
New Delhi Shanghai Taipei Toronto

With offices in

Argentina Austria Brazil Chile Czech Republic France Greece
Guatemala Hungary Italy Japan Poland Portugal Singapore
South Korea Switzerland Thailand Turkey Ukraine Vietnam

OXFORD and OXFORD ENGLISH are registered trade marks of
Oxford University Press in the UK and in certain other countries

© Oxford University Press 2010

The moral rights of the author have been asserted

Database right Oxford University Press (maker)

First published in Oxford Bookworms 2010
20

No unauthorized photocopying

All rights reserved. No part of this publication may be reproduced,
stored in a retrieval system, or transmitted, in any form or by any means,
without the prior permission in writing of Oxford University Press,
or as expressly permitted by law, or under terms agreed with the appropriate
reprographics rights organization. Enquiries concerning reproduction
outside the scope of the above should be sent to the ELT Rights Department,
Oxford University Press, at the address above

You must not circulate this book in any other binding or cover
and you must impose this same condition on any acquirer

Any websites referred to in this publication are in the public domain and
their addresses are provided by Oxford University Press for information only.
Oxford University Press disclaims any responsibility for the content

ISBN: 978 0 19 423780 2

A complete recording of this Bookworms edition of
Gandhi is available.

Printed in China

This book is printed on paper from certified and well-managed sources.

Word count (main text): 17,000

For more information on the Oxford Bookworms Library,
visit www.oup.com/elt/gradedreaders

ACKNOWLEDGEMENTS

Illustration page 7 by: Peter Bull

The publishers would like to thank the following for their kind permission to reproduce images:

Alamy Images pp35 (Amritsar Massacre Memorial/imagebroker), 44 (Mahatma Gandhi breaking the salt law/ Dinodia Images), 73 (Raj Ghat Memorial/Moreleaze Travel India); Camera Press p39 (Gandhi released from prison/Photograph by Keystone - France, Camera Press London); GandhiServe pp iv (Walking from Segaon to Wardha, 1933/Counsic Brothers), 2 (Gandhi's birthplace/Vithalbhai Jhaveri), 3 (Gandhi, age 7/Vithalbhai Jhaveri), 8 (Mahatma Gandhi, 1895/Vithalbhai Jhaveri), 14 (Indian Ambulance Corps/Vithalbhai Jhaveri), 15 (Kasturba Gandhi with her four sons/Vithalbhai Jhaveri), 17 (In front of his office, 1905/Vithalbhai Jhaveri), 18 (Settlers of Phoenix Settlement/Vithalbhai Jhaveri), 21 (Recuperating from assault, 1908/Vithalbhai Jhaveri), 23 (On Tolstoi Farm, ca. 1910/Isa Sarid), 24 (Policeman confronting Gandhi, 1913/Local History Museum), 27 (Consultation with friends, 1913/Vithalbhai Jhaveri), 29 (Kasturba and Mahatma Gandhi's building/Eduard Friedl), 41 (Addressing a meeting, 1926/Vithalbhai Jhaveri), 46 (After landing in England, 1931/Vithalbhai Jhaveri), 47 (With textile workers, 1931/Vithalbhai Jhaveri), 52 (Walking in the countryside, 1938/Kanu Gandhi), 54 (With secretary Mahadev Desai, 1939/Kanu Gandhi), 57 (With M.A. Jinnah, 1944/ Vithalbhai Jhaveri), 59 (Sharing a joke with Nehru, 1946/Vithalbhai Jhaveri), 60 (Walking in Noakhali, 1946/ Vithalbhai Jhaveri), 63 (During march through Bihar, 1947/Jagan Mehta), 71 (The last journey, 1948/Vithalbhai Jhaveri); Getty Images p 31 (Pandit Jawaharlal Nehru/Popperfoto); TopFoto pp10 (West Street, abt 1900/Roger-Viollet), 35 (General Dyer/Topham Picturepoint), 36 (Gandhi on the spinning wheel/Topham Picturepoint), 51 (Muhammad Ali Jinnah), 56 (Gandhi with his son Devdas/Topham/Dinodia), 62 (Gandhi with Lord and Lady Mountbatten/World History Archive), 64 (Gandhi with the prime minister of Burma/Topham/Dinodia); Wikimedia Commons pp28 (Gandhi back in India, 1915), 38 (Central Prison Yeravda).

CONTENTS

1 From India to England (1869–1892)

When Mohandas Karamchand Gandhi died in 1948, he was one of the most famous men in the world: leaders from many countries spoke about him, and people all over the world felt sad because he had died. Today, people everywhere still recognize his face. His words are still read and many books have been written about his life. Today, when world leaders visit India, they take flowers to the Raj Ghat in Delhi, where Gandhi's body lay after his death more than sixty years ago.

Gandhi believed that people could change the world without using violence. For many years he worked with others to free India from the British, and in the end he was successful. All his life, he worked to help poor people. He lived a simple but extraordinary life and he became the leader of many.

The British had first come to India in the seventeenth century, but the British Empire only began to control the whole of India in the nineteenth century. India was a very large country, with many provinces, cities, languages, and customs, and Indian kings worked with the British to govern the country.

Gandhi was born on 2 October 1869 in Porbandar, a very old town in the province of Gujarat. About 15,000 people lived in this small town on India's western coast. A wall of white stone had been built along the beach because the sea was often rough. There were many fishing boats and beautiful sea birds to watch.

Gandhi's father, Karamchand, lived with his family in a large, very old house made of white stone. Mohandas was the youngest child – he had an older sister and two older brothers. They all spoke Gujarati, the language of that part of India, and, like most people there, they belonged to the Hindu faith.

Gandhi's birthplace

When Mohandas was seven years old, his father was given a job in Rajkot, where the British government had its central offices for the province of Gujarat. And so the family moved to Rajkot, about 190 kilometres east, away from the sea. It was another old city, with narrow streets, and Mohandas started to go to school there.

Mohandas was a very shy boy, afraid of ghosts and of the dark. His mother, Putlibai, taught him to pray, to help him with these fears. In those days, different groups in India lived separately, and were not allowed to be friends with each other. One group had a very difficult life; they were known at that time as Untouchables. They were given the dirtiest jobs to do, and were not allowed to use the same buildings as other people. Mohandas argued about this with his mother. He did not understand why some people had to live separately. He went to school with Muslims and Hindus, boys with different faiths, and from childhood he dreamed that all people could be friends.

Gandhi at the age of 7

Mohandas and his brothers and sister were not allowed to eat meat, to drink wine, or to smoke, because of their Hindu faith. But secretly, Mohandas and his brother Karsandas began to smoke cigarettes, and later he copied a school friend and began to eat meat. But because of his love for his mother, he soon stopped both eating meat and smoking cigarettes.

In 1882, when Mohandas was thirteen years old, he was married to Kastur Kapadia, who was also thirteen years old. In those days, marriage of children was the custom in India. His brother Karsandas, who was two years older, was also married at the same time. Mohandas accepted this arrangement – he felt happy because of the music, the new clothes, and the rich food at the wedding. But much later, he became an enemy of child marriages and worked hard to stop them.

During the first years of their marriage, Kastur usually lived with her parents. Mohandas soon began to love his wife, but it was a stormy marriage at first. Kastur was a confident girl, and Mohandas felt jealous of her because he was still very shy. He tried to control her, and then he felt ashamed of himself.

Gandhi's father, Karamchand, became very ill soon after the wedding, and Mohandas helped to look after him. For three years, he cared for his father every day after school. One night in 1885 Mohandas left his father's room to go and be with Kastur, and a few minutes later his father died. Gandhi always felt ashamed that he was not with his father when he died.

After Karamchand Gandhi's death, the family had less money. Laxmidas, the oldest brother, was now the head of the family. Mohandas finished school and began to dream about going to London to study law. Although he was still very shy, he was not afraid of new experiences. His oldest son, Harilal, was born in 1888 and Kastur wanted Mohandas to stay with them. His mother did not want him to leave India either, until Mohandas promised her that he would not touch meat, wine, or women. Although many friends of the family disagreed with Mohandas's plan, Laxmidas managed to find enough money for it.

Mohandas bought his ticket and western clothes, and in

September 1888 he said goodbye to his family and boarded the *Clyde*. The voyage was three weeks long, through the Suez Canal and across the Mediterranean Sea. On the ship Mohandas refused to eat meat. Other passengers warned him that he would need to eat meat in London because of the cold weather, but Mohandas remembered his promise to his mother.

In London, Mohandas met other Indian students. By 1888, more than 100 Indians had studied law in London, but Mohandas was the first from Porbandar. He felt very shy and he did not like the food. Soon, he discovered a vegetarian restaurant called the Central where he enjoyed the food. He began to read vegetarian books and became interested in different foods. He decided that he would never eat meat again – and he never did.

At first, Mohandas had dancing and music lessons, but they were too expensive. He began to cook for himself and to walk everywhere in order to save money. He went to vegetarian meetings and became friends with some British Christians. He also met Annie Besant, a famous writer who worked to help poor people in London, and who was interested in the Hindu faith.

For the first time he became interested in God, and he began to search for the truth about God. He wanted to learn about different ideas about God, and he began to read in English the *Bhagavad Gita* (the Song of God), which is one of the holy books of the Hindu faith. He had never read this book in his first language, Gujarati. He began to read the holy books of the Jews and Christians, and he also went to meetings with Indians of the Muslim faith.

Mohandas finished his studies after three years in London, and returned to India in 1891. Laxmidas met the ship in Bombay, now called Mumbai, and told Mohandas that their mother had died earlier that year. Mohandas was filled with sadness. He was unable to tell her that he had kept his promise while he had been in London.

Mohandas was happy to be with his family. He played with Harilal and the children of Laxmidas and went for walks with them. Laxmidas hoped that Mohandas was going to earn lots of money as a lawyer, but it was not easy. First, Mohandas went to Bombay which was the biggest city in western India, 940 kilometres south of Porbandar. He began to learn about Indian law, but there were many good lawyers in Bombay and no one wanted to use him. He was still very shy and he hated going to court.

Mohandas went back to Rajkot and opened his own law office there. He began to find some easy work, but in 1893 his life changed again. His brother Laxmidas got into trouble with a British officer called Ollivant. Because Mohandas had met Ollivant in London, Laxmidas asked Mohandas to go and talk to him. At first Mohandas refused, but at last his brother persuaded him. Ollivant remembered Mohandas, but he did not like Laxmidas. He became angry when Mohandas tried to talk to him. He called his servant who pushed Mohandas out of the room.

This was a painful experience and Mohandas felt angry and bitter with himself, as well as with the British officer. For the first time he realized how strong the British government was. An older Indian lawyer told Mohandas to forget the experience, but most of Mohandas's work was in Ollivant's court and he felt miserable and helpless.

Just then Laxmidas received a letter from a company in Porbandar. The company had an office in the city of Durban, in South Africa. Abdullah Sheth, the head of the Durban office, could not speak English and he needed someone to help him to work with the company lawyers. Gandhi was happy to go to South Africa for a year. Although he would not have his own office, he would visit a new country, meet new people, and have different experiences. He would also be able to repay to Laxmidas the money he had given him for his studies in London.

Mohandas had been back in India for two years, and once again he prepared to leave. He said goodbye again to Kastur and their two sons (Manilal had been born in 1892) and travelled to Bombay. In April 1893, he boarded the *Safari* and began the long voyage to South Africa.

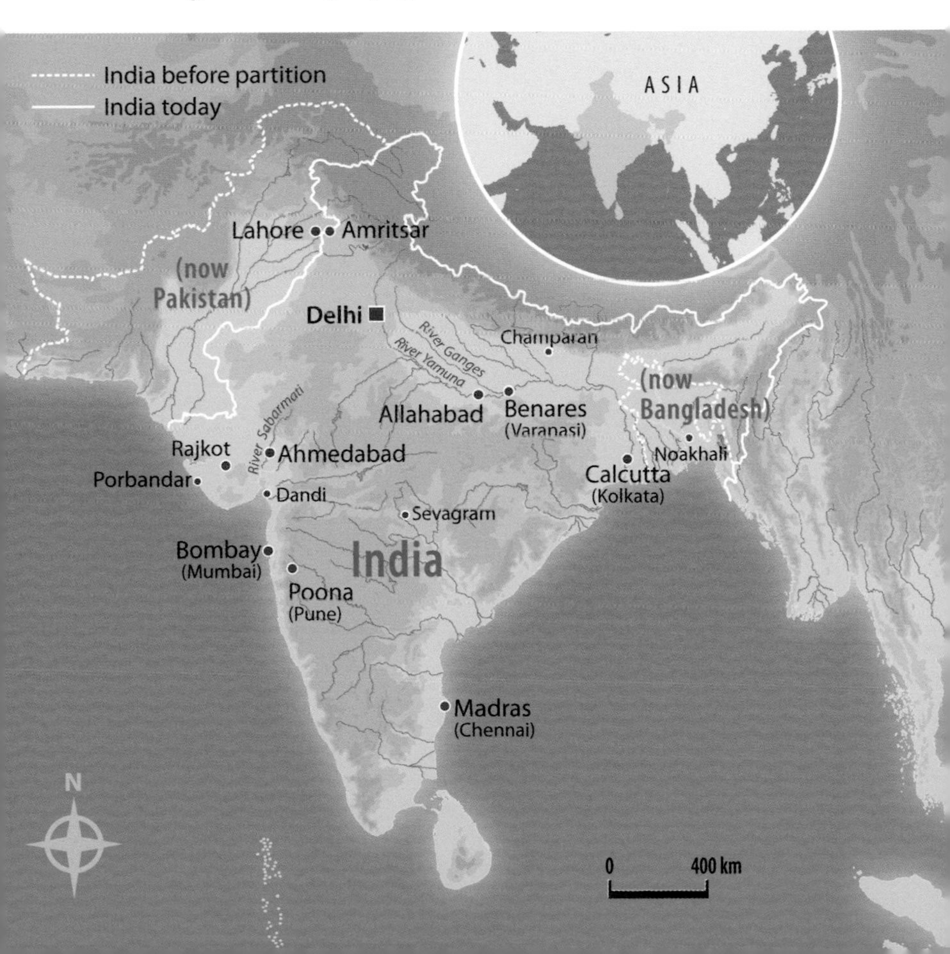

2 South Africa (1893–1894)

After five weeks, Mohandas Gandhi arrived in Durban, on the east coast of South Africa. In 1893, South Africa was not one nation, but several separate provinces. Durban was in the province of Natal, which was part of the British Empire. The British had large sugar and coffee farms in Natal and from 1860 the British had been bringing farm workers from India to work on these farms. The Indian farm workers were very poor and they were not allowed to leave the farms until they had worked there for five years.

Durban was the biggest city in Natal. About 30,000 people lived in the city. Half of them were white people, one quarter were Indian, and one quarter were African. There were some Indian shops and businesses, many of which were owned by Muslims.

Abdullah Sheth owned several ships and businesses and was very rich. He was surprised when he met Gandhi, who was wearing an expensive black suit with a pocket watch as well as a black turban. It was unusual to see a suit and a turban together, because at that time Muslim Indians wore long clothes and large turbans while Christian Indians wore western clothes.

Gandhi in South Africa, 1895

Abdullah Sheth took Gandhi to the Durban court, with his white lawyer. The judge stared at Gandhi and finally told him to take off his turban. Mohandas refused and left the court. The next day a newspaper reported this story, and called Gandhi an 'unwelcome visitor'. Gandhi wrote to the newspaper and explained that the turban was an important part of his Indian life. Gandhi continued to wear his turban while he lived in South Africa. Abdullah Sheth began to understand Gandhi, and he told him about the difficult life of the Indians in South Africa.

Abdullah Sheth had had an argument with an Indian who owed him a lot of money. The man lived in Pretoria, the capital of the Transvaal province. This province was not part of the British Empire at that time, and it had its own white government. Abdullah Sheth asked Gandhi to go to Pretoria to work with his lawyers there, to try to get the money.

After only a week in Durban, Gandhi bought his train ticket and began the long journey to Pretoria. He bought himself a first-class ticket in order to have a seat in a comfortable compartment on the train. The train stopped at Pietermaritzburg, the capital of Natal, and a white passenger got into the compartment where Gandhi was sitting. He looked at Gandhi and then called the guards, who asked Gandhi to move out of the first-class compartment because he was not white. Gandhi refused. He explained that he had a first-class ticket and that he had been allowed to get into the compartment in Durban.

'You must leave the compartment or we shall call the police,' the guards said. Gandhi still refused, and the police pushed him off the train with his luggage.

Gandhi went to the station waiting room. It was 9 p.m. and there was no light in the room. It was dark and

Durban, in 1900

extremely cold. Gandhi sat alone all night, thinking about what had happened and about his future. He was twenty-three years old. Should he go back to India, or should he stay and fight against injustice? He realized that the injustice he was experiencing was caused by deep racism. That night, in the station at Pietermaritzburg, Gandhi decided that he was prepared to fight against racism.

When he finally reached Pretoria the next evening it was dark and Gandhi did not know where to stay. An African American offered to take him to a small hotel. The owner gave Gandhi a room. 'But you must eat in your room,' he said. 'The other people here are white and they could be angry if you eat in the restaurant.' Gandhi told the owner that he was beginning to understand conditions in South Africa. But later, the owner came back. 'Please come and eat in the restaurant,' he said. 'The others do not mind.'

One day in Pretoria, Gandhi was pushed off the path by a white guard. Only white people were allowed to walk on the paths: Africans and Indians had to walk in the roads.

And so Gandhi, through painful experiences like these, discovered that he wanted to fight injustice. He quickly changed from a shy young man to a confident one.

In Pretoria, Gandhi met the Indian who owed Abdullah Sheth money. Gandhi realized that they would both lose a lot of money if they went to court, and he persuaded them to end their argument without doing so. This result made Gandhi very happy. He realized that he wanted to bring enemies together by working towards agreement between them, not by going to court. He believed that this should be the real work of a lawyer.

While in Pretoria, Gandhi called a meeting of all Indians living there, and he began to teach English to some of them. He continued to read about different faiths. He became friends with Abdullah Sheth's lawyer, who was a Christian. Abdullah Sheth loved the Muslim faith and the *Qur'an*, the holy book of the Muslims. He talked to Gandhi about his faith, and Gandhi read the *Qur'an*. Some of Gandhi's friends wanted him to change his faith, but he wanted all faiths to grow.

Gandhi had finished the work for Abdullah Sheth and he was ready to go back to India when he read about the government's plan to take away the vote from Indians in Natal. Abdullah Sheth and his friends asked Gandhi if he would stay in South Africa in order to fight against this new law. Gandhi agreed, and immediately started work.

He called a meeting and asked all Indians in South Africa to sign a letter against the new law. The letter was signed by 10,000 people, and Gandhi sent copies to newspapers in India and in England, as well as to the government in Natal. All Indians in South Africa joined Gandhi – the poor farm workers and the rich men of business, Muslims, Hindus, and Christians.

In May 1894, in Abdullah Sheth's house, the Natal Indian Congress was born. Gandhi chose this name because he had read about the Indian National Congress, which had been working to change laws in India since 1885.

At the age of twenty-five, Gandhi had become a leader.

3 Experiences of violence (1895–1898)

One day a poor Indian farm worker called Balasundaram came to Gandhi's office. Balasundaram was crying. He had been beaten by his rich employer. His teeth were broken and his mouth was bleeding. It was always a mystery to Gandhi that people could injure other human beings. Gandhi sent Balasundaram to a doctor and took the doctor's report to court. Gandhi managed to persuade the court to move Balasundaram to another employer. Because he was willing to help them, many poor farm workers came to Gandhi and news of his work reached India.

In 1896 Gandhi sailed to India to fetch his family. After a voyage of twenty-four days, he arrived in Calcutta, now called Kolkata, the capital of the British government in India. He travelled 2,000 kilometres by train across India to his family in Rajkot.

But although Gandhi was happy to see his family, he did not spend all his time with them. He arranged meetings in Bombay, Calcutta, Poona, now called Pune, and Madras, now called Chennai, in order to speak to people about the conditions of Indians in South Africa. Indian newspapers wrote about Gandhi and these meetings.

While he was staying in Rajkot, there was great fear that a serious diseasc would come to the city from Bombay. Gandhi joined a group which visited the very poorest parts of Rajkot. He was always very interested in preventing disease, and preferred the work of a nurse to the work of a lawyer. His sister's husband was very ill at this time, and Gandhi brought him to his house, where he could look after him.

But Gandhi was only in India for a few months before Abdullah Sheth asked him to return to South Africa. This time, Gandhi travelled with Kastur and their two sons. They sailed from Bombay on one of Abdullah Sheth's ships, and arrived in Durban in December 1896.

Many of the white people of Durban had heard about the meetings which Gandhi had organized in India. These meetings had made South Africa unpopular in India and so the people of Durban did not want Gandhi to return to the city. The passengers were prevented from leaving the ship. They were kept on the ship for twenty-three days, but at last they were allowed to leave.

Gandhi was recognized and a crowd of young white men began to follow him and to throw stones at him. They hit him and kicked him and pulled off his turban. The brave wife of the police chief was passing in the street and she came up to Gandhi. The crowd stepped back because they did not want to hurt a woman, and soon the police arrived. Gandhi was taken to a friend's house where he was looked after. Gandhi refused to take the young men to court for their violence against him, and this made some of the white people feel ashamed.

For the next few years Gandhi lived with his family in a pleasant house near the beach. Two more sons were born: Ramdas in 1898 and Devadas in 1900. Gandhi continued to work for the Indians and to help the poor farm workers. Every day he also worked as a nurse in a small hospital, giving medicine to sick workers.

Two groups of white people lived in South Africa: those

from Britain who spoke English, and those from Holland who were known as Afrikaners and spoke Afrikaans, a kind of Dutch. The British and the Afrikaners hated each other, and when gold was discovered in the Afrikaner province of Transvaal in 1899, a war started between them.

Gandhi decided to help the British. At that time he believed that the British Empire was a good government. He called together a group of more than 1,000 Indians to help care for soldiers who were wounded during the war. This group was called the Ambulance Corps and for six weeks the group carried the dead and wounded to safety, sometimes for distances of more than 30 kilometres. In Natal and in England, newspapers reported the work of Gandhi's Ambulance Corps.

Gandhi with the Ambulance Corps

After the war, Gandhi believed that his work in South Africa was over and he went back to India with his family. He went to Calcutta for the yearly meeting of the Indian National Congress and began to meet other Indian leaders.

He stayed with Gopal Gokhale, an important leader, who thought that Gandhi would soon be a leader in India. At the Congress meeting, Gandhi spoke for a few minutes about South Africa. He helped in one of the offices, and he also helped some Untouchables with the dirty job of cleaning the toilets.

After the Indian National Congress meeting Gandhi went back to Rajkot by train, stopping at several cities in order to learn more about India. (The first railways were built in India in 1853, and by 1880 there were 14,500 kilometres of railway across India.) Gandhi decided to travel as a third-class passenger. The third-class compartments were dirty and noisy and Gandhi began to experience the difficulties that poor people lived with in India.

Gokhale wanted Gandhi to work with him in Bombay, but Gandhi remembered that he had failed in Bombay in 1894 and so he opened a law office in Rajkot. Gandhi was earning enough money for a comfortable life, and he and his family enjoyed living in Rajkot. But in November 1902 Gandhi received this message from South Africa: 'Mr Chamberlain is expected here. Please return immediately.'

So Gandhi left his wife and his four sons, and returned to South Africa. He had been in India for only one year.

Kastur Gandhi with their four sons

4 Wars and books (1899–1910)

Joseph Chamberlain, a British leader, was visiting South Africa in order to collect money for the British government. Gandhi prepared reports for him about the problems of the Indians in South Africa, but Chamberlain was not interested. After the war, many Indians wanted to return to their homes and jobs in the Transvaal province, but British officers made this difficult. Gandhi decided to stay in the Transvaal to help the Indians there, and he opened a law office in Johannesburg.

Gandhi helped to start a new weekly newspaper called *Indian Opinion*, and he wrote for it every week. This was the beginning of his regular newspaper writing, which continued for the rest of his life.

At this time, Gandhi began to read the *Gita* seriously. Every day he learned some words from it, and slowly his opinion about money changed. Instead of earning money for himself and his family, he wanted his money to help other people outside his family.

Gandhi often ate his meals at a vegetarian restaurant, and there he met a British newspaper reporter called Henry Polak. They became friends, and one day in 1904, when Gandhi went by train to the offices of the *Indian Opinion* in Durban, Polak gave him a book to read on the long journey. The book was *Unto This Last* by John Ruskin, a famous British writer and thinker, and Gandhi found it impossible to put the book down. Gandhi discovered some of his deepest beliefs in this book: that every human being has the right to earn enough money to live comfortably; that everyone should do some work with their hands; and that the work of a cook, for example, is as valuable as the work of a lawyer. Gandhi decided to change his life, and begin to live in a simpler way.

Gandhi at his office with Henry Polak (left)

Immediately, Gandhi moved the offices of *Indian Opinion* to a farm in Phoenix, about 22 kilometres from Durban. All the newspaper's workers went to live on the farm, but Gandhi kept his office in Johannesburg where Henry Polak began to work with him.

Kastur had come to South Africa in 1902, with three of their boys. (Harilal, the eldest, stayed with his uncle in Rajkot.) Gandhi now explained to his wife that they were going to live differently: the servant lived as one of the family, and they all helped with the cooking, washing, and cleaning. When Henry Polak, who was a Jew, married a Christian woman called Millie, they came to live with the Gandhi family and helped with the work of the house.

In 1906, African Zulus in the British province of Natal began to fight against the government because of a new tax. Gandhi offered to start an Ambulance Corps to help injured soldiers, as he had done in 1899. White people did not want to care for the Zulus, and so for four weeks, Gandhi and his ambulance team cared for injured Zulus.

Gandhi experienced the horror of war, and wrote later about the 'terrible cruelty of the British soldiers'. Sometimes

The people of Phoenix Farm

the corps marched for over 60 kilometres a day through the beautiful hills, and Gandhi had time to think deeply about many things. He realized that his heart was with the Zulus, not with the British, and that he wanted to give his life to helping others. He knew that there would not be time for a normal family life, and he did not want more children. After he had discussed this with his wife, they began to sleep separately.

After the war, Gandhi moved his family from their comfortable home in Johannesburg to the farm in Phoenix. There were now several families living there. They worked and cooked together, and earned the same money: £3 each month.

The government of the Transvaal now wanted every Indian over eight years old to give their names and personal details to the government and to carry papers at all times. Police officers would be able to stop Indians, or go inside their houses, to check their papers.

Gandhi arranged a meeting in a theatre in Johannesburg in the Transvaal to discuss these laws with other Indians, Muslims and Hindus. The theatre was full of people who were angry about the new laws. When Gandhi asked them, everyone stood up and promised God that they would fight against these laws. They were all ready to follow Gandhi.

Before the new laws could begin, the British government had to agree to them. And so in October 1906 Gandhi sailed to London, where he met many British leaders. With the help of some students, Gandhi wrote about 5,000 letters during his six weeks there, explaining the situation to newspapers and leaders. The British government promised Gandhi that the new laws would not be accepted – but at the same time, they told the Transvaal that they *would* accept the laws.

When Gandhi returned to South Africa, he learned that the British government had lied to him. In 1907, Transvaal became independent, and at once the new laws against Indians began.

Gandhi realized that small groups could not defeat a strong government. He thought about a new way of fighting against laws without using violence. He called this new way *satyagraha*, a name made of two words: *satya*, which means truth, and *agraha* which means force. Gandhi believed that truth and love would change the world in a way that violence could not.

Most Indians refused to give their names to the government, and the police began to arrest the Indian leaders. More than 150 Indians were put in prison because they refused to obey the new laws. Gandhi was sent to prison in Johannesburg for two months. The food was bad and the place was dirty, but the guards were friendly and Gandhi was allowed to read. He read the *Gita* in the morning, and the *Qur'an* in the evening, and he was happy to have many other books.

The leader of the government, Jan Christiaan Smuts, sent a message to Gandhi in prison: if the Indians agreed to give their names to the government, the new laws would be taken away. Gandhi agreed to this, and was released from prison in January 1908.

He immediately arranged a meeting with other Indians. Many agreed with Gandhi, but some who were angry with Gandhi followed him after the meeting and beat him with sticks. Gandhi was badly injured and for ten days he was cared for in the home of white Christians. The daughter of this family sang a famous Christian song to Gandhi called 'Lead kindly light'. Gandhi often remembered one line from this song: 'one step enough for me'.

Gandhi after the beating, 1908

Indians began to give their names to the government, as Gandhi advised, but in May 1908 the government said that the laws would stay. Smuts had lied to Gandhi.

Gandhi continued to work with other Indians, and at a meeting in Johannesburg in August 1908 they decided to burn their government papers. Gandhi was again sent to prison. This time, with the other Indian prisoners, he had to break stones, cook, and sew the prison hats which were worn by the prisoners.

While he was in prison, Kastur became seriously ill. 'I love you so much,' wrote Gandhi, 'that even if you die, you will still be alive to me.' She was still ill when he came out of prison, and he cared for her at Phoenix Farm.

But he was soon in prison again. About 4,000 Indians were sent to prison in 1908 and 1909. The families of many prisoners went to live on the Phoenix farm, where Maganlal Gandhi (the son of Gandhi's cousin) had become a leader of the farm.

Harilal, Gandhi's oldest son, had married in 1906 and come to South Africa with his wife. Harilal joined Gandhi's work, and was sent to prison several times.

In 1909, Gandhi went to London again, but the British government was unwilling to disagree with Smuts. On the ship back to South Africa, Gandhi wrote a book in which he described the changes he wanted in India. He wanted Indians to govern India and to refuse to live a western life. He wanted rich Indians to live a simple life. He believed that Hindus, Muslims, and other faiths belonged to one Indian nation, and that non-violence was central to Indian life: Indians should not copy the violence of the British.

Gandhi sent a copy of the book to the great Russian writer, Leo Tolstoy, who wrote the famous book *War and Peace*. Tolstoy believed that people should refuse to obey a bad government. He hated war and violence and believed that a simple, holy life was the best for everyone. In 1894, Gandhi had read one of Tolstoy's books, which helped him develop his ideas. Tolstoy read Gandhi's book, and wrote several letters to Gandhi, just before he died in 1910.

When Gandhi arrived back in South Africa, he realized that it was too difficult to look after so many families at Phoenix Farm, which was too far from his office in Johannesburg. It was time to move again.

5 Marching for change (1910–1914)

Gandhi had become good friends with Hermann Kallenbach, a German Jew who was interested in different faiths and who was looking for ways to live a simple, peaceful life. They had first met in 1906 and Gandhi had stayed with Kallenbach when he was working in Johannesburg.

In 1910, Kallenbach gave Gandhi more than 400 hectares of land, about 35 kilometres from Johannesburg. It was good land, with its own water and many fruit trees, and they decided to call it Tolstoy Farm. Kallenbach organized simple houses which were built by the families. About seventy-five people lived there: Hindus, Muslims, and Christians. There were no servants, and everyone helped with the cooking, cleaning, and washing. They ate only vegetarian food, and Gandhi made the bread. Everyone wore simple clothes and

Tolstoy Farm

Kallenbach learned to make shoes. The families always travelled third-class on the trains, and often walked to Johannesburg. Sometimes Gandhi and Kallenbach walked the 35 kilometres to the office in Johannesburg, and back again on the same day.

In 1910, the different provinces in South Africa joined together to make the nation of South Africa, a nation with a white government although about 70 per cent of the people who lived there were black.

At this time the most important problem for Indian workers was a £3 yearly tax which they had to pay to the government. Gandhi worked to try to end this tax.

Harilal became angry with his father because Gandhi sent a cousin to study in London but refused to allow his son to go. In the end, Harilal went back to India with his family in 1911.

In 1913, the government decided that Hindu marriages and Muslim marriages were unacceptable: only Christian marriages were accepted by the courts. Indian men and women were extremely angry about this new law and Gandhi started a new fight against the government. His plan was for large numbers of people to disobey the law. If there was not

A policeman stops Gandhi as he leads the march, 1913

enough room for them all in the prisons, things would be very difficult for the government.

Kastur and a group of women went into the Transvaal province without papers and were arrested and sent to prison. Indian factory workers stopped working. When Indian miners joined the strike, they had to leave their homes which belonged to their employers. Gandhi asked the 5,000 miners to walk 290 kilometres with him – from Natal, into Transvaal and on to Johannesburg, where they could live at Tolstoy Farm.

Gandhi told the miners that they must remain calm and peaceful. If some of them were arrested, the others would continue to march. There must be no violence.

Gandhi phoned Smuts before he started the march, but Smuts refused to speak to him. On 6 November 1913, the march began. Gandhi was arrested a few days later and sent to prison. The marchers continued, led by Polak and Kallenbach, who were later arrested too. The marchers walked about 170 kilometres before the government sent soldiers to put the marchers on trains back to Natal. The soldiers beat many of the marchers, and some of them died. But more and more Indians joined the strike, and every detail was reported in Indian and British newspapers.

After six weeks, Smuts sent a message to Gandhi in prison: he was ready to talk. Gandhi and other leaders were released in December 1913, and when Gandhi spoke at a large meeting in Durban, he wore the simple white clothes of the poor Indian workers.

Gandhi had been helped by gifts of money from India and from a new British friend, Charles Freer Andrews. Andrews was a Christian who had met Rabindranath Tagore, the great Indian writer, in London in 1912. In January 1914,

Andrews went to South Africa to help Gandhi with *Indian Opinion*. He gave Gandhi all his money, and became one of Gandhi's closest friends.

Gandhi negotiated with Smuts for six months, and finally, in June 1914, agreement was reached. The £3 tax was stopped, and Indian marriages were accepted. Indians, however, were unable to move from one province to another. The agreement was not a complete success, but it showed the world that non-violence could be effective.

Some of the rich Indians in South Africa were disappointed because Gandhi had failed to help them, but the poor Indians loved him. They had called him *bhai* (brother) for a number of years, but now they began to call him *Mahatma* (which means great soul), though Gandhi was never happy with this name. Kastur was now called Kasturba (Kastur-mother).

Kasturba became very ill after she was released from prison. While Gandhi was caring for her, he received news that his brother Laxmidas had died in Porbandar. Laxmidas had been angry because Gandhi had not become a rich, successful lawyer. But before he died, Laxmidas wrote to Gandhi saying that he wanted to visit him in South Africa. Karsandas, the third brother, had died in Rajkot in 1913.

Gokhale, who had visited Gandhi in South Africa in 1912, persuaded Gandhi to return to live in India. He believed that Gandhi could become an important leader there. Gokhale was ill in London and asked Gandhi to visit him there before going on to India.

The families from the Tolstoy Farm had already sailed for India when in July 1914 Gandhi left South Africa for the last time, sailing to London with Kasturba and Kallenbach.

While they were on the ship, the First World War started, and as soon as he reached London, Gandhi began to organize an Ambulance Corps. However, he became seriously ill and his doctor told him to return to India. His German friend Kallenbach was not allowed to travel with him, however, because the British government in India considered Germans to be enemies. Sadly, he said goodbye to Gandhi and went back to South Africa.

Kasturba and Gandhi sailed for India in December 1914. Gandhi's experiences in South Africa had made him confident, and he had learned that he could organize and lead others. He took with him the lessons he had learned in South Africa: about the simple life, about the disease of racism, and about how non-violence could change laws. His faith in God and his love for human beings had led him to a life of bravery and self-control.

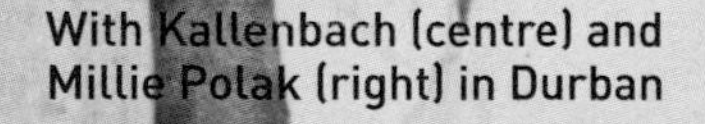

With Kallenbach (centre) and Millie Polak (right) in Durban

6 Return to India (1915–1919)

Gandhi and Kasturba arrived in Bombay in January 1915. It was twelve years since Gandhi had been in India. A crowd met the ship, because his work in South Africa had made him famous. A party was arranged for him and other Indian leaders. Gandhi had decided that he would never wear western clothes again and he looked very different from the other leaders, who were wearing expensive clothes. Gandhi wore a turban and long Indian clothes like a poor man. When he began travelling regularly by train, he began wearing a cheap hat instead of a turban. He now always travelled in third-class compartments.

Gandhi's return to India

The *ashram* in Ahmedabad

Maganlal Gandhi and Charles Andrews were leading the Tolstoy Farm group until Gandhi arrived. They were staying at Tagore's school, near Calcutta, until they found their own place.

Gandhi decided to live near Ahmedabad, which was a rich, old city and the capital of the British province of Gujarat. There were textile factories in the city, but it had been a centre of spinning, and Gandhi was interested in the old way of spinning cotton.

Gandhi was given land beside the River Sabarmati and the group of about twenty-five people moved into low white houses there. Gandhi lived in a small room, and slept outside even when it was very cold. But life there was not peaceful for long. Gandhi invited a young family from the Untouchable group to come and live in the *ashram*. This was unpopular with many of Gandhi's friends, and at first Kasturba and Maganlal Gandhi were also unhappy about it.

The *ashram* depended on gifts of money from rich Indians, and now these gifts stopped. One day, all the money had gone. Then a rich young man came with a generous gift of money, because he had always wanted Untouchables to live with other groups. (Today, the name Untouchable is unacceptable in India. People from that group are now called Dalits.)

In February 1916, Gandhi was invited to speak at the new Hindu university in Benares, also called Varanasi, and one of the holiest cities in India, beside the River Ganges. Annie Besant, the famous English woman that Gandhi had met in London when he was a student, had moved to India in 1893. The university had developed from a school she had started in Benares. She invited the rich and famous, British and Indian, the old kings and the new leaders, to come to a meeting at the new university.

When Gandhi stood up to speak, he looked round at the expensive clothes of the people sitting in front of him. He told them they must change the way they lived. He spoke of the dirty cities he had seen, and of his journeys in third-class compartments with the poor people of India. India would be saved not by doctors and lawyers, he said, but by farmers. Many people in the room became angry. 'Sit down, Gandhi!' some shouted, and others began to leave the room. Gandhi had to stop speaking.

At that time other Indian leaders were more important than Gandhi, but people realized that Gandhi was unusual. His clothes and his life in the *ashram* were different. Also, he usually spoke and wrote in Gujarati, not English, and he learned to speak other Indian languages too. He wanted all leaders to use Indian languages instead of English.

Gandhi began to speak at the conferences of the Indian National Congress. Vallabhbhai Patel, a successful lawyer in Ahmedabad, had laughed about Gandhi's opinions. But at a conference in 1916, Patel listened to Gandhi with interest.

Jawaharlal Nehru

Later that year, at a conference in Lucknow in the north of India, another important person came into Gandhi's life: the young lawyer Jawaharlal Nehru. He was the son of Motilal Nehru, a rich lawyer and Congress leader from Kashmir in the far north of India. He had been to school and university in Britain and he thought Gandhi was 'very distant and very different'.

At the same conference Gandhi also met Raj Kumar Shukla, a poor farm worker from nearby Champaran in Bihar province. He told Gandhi about the problems of the Champaran farmers, and asked Gandhi to help them. After some time, Gandhi agreed to go to Champaran, and it was here that Gandhi's first real work in India began.

Most of the land in Champaran was owned by the British, but the farmers were Indian. The problem for the farmers was indigo, a plant used in textile factories to dye material blue. The owners made the farmers grow indigo, but they could not get a good price for it, so they were extremely poor.

No one knew Gandhi in Champaran, but the poor farmers welcomed him, and Gandhi decided to stay and help them. The landowners were unhappy about his work, and the government asked him to leave. He refused and was told to come to court. A large crowd of poor farmers waited outside the court. Later, Gandhi wrote that 'in this meeting with the [poor farmers] I was face to face with God, *ahimsa*, truth'.

Gandhi told the court that he would not obey the order to leave, because he was obeying a higher law. The government decided not to put him in prison and he was allowed to stay in Champaran. All over India, newspapers reported Gandhi's refusal to obey the government.

Several lawyers working in Champaran joined Gandhi, and some of them became his followers. Mahadev Desai, a lawyer and writer, joined Gandhi and worked with him for the rest of his life. Rajendra Prasad and J B Kriplani, who later became important leaders, also left their comfortable lives and joined Gandhi in Champaran. There they slept on the ground, ate simple food, and washed their own clothes. They walked from village to village to collect information from the farm workers about their situation, which Gandhi needed for his report.

Kasturba and others from the *ashram* came to live in Champaran to help the poor women and children on the farms. Gandhi talked to many farmers. He met teachers and doctors, and also the landowners, and he wrote to newspapers about everything he saw.

In October 1917, the government agreed that the farmers could stop growing indigo. Gandhi had succeeded and his name was now famous in India.

Gandhi stayed in Champaran, helping the farmers, but in March 1918 the workers in the textile factories in Ahmedabad asked him to help them. And so he returned to the *ashram*. For a long time the textile workers had been asking the factory owners for more money, but the owners had refused. Although some of the factory owners were friends with Gandhi, he wanted to help the workers. He suggested a strike, and the workers stopped work.

After two weeks, the owners still refused to pay more money, and the workers were becoming hungry. Gandhi decided that he would stop eating until the factory owners agreed to negotiate. Gandhi fasted for four days, eating nothing and drinking only water. The owners began to negotiate with their workers, because they did not want Gandhi to become ill. At last, an agreement was reached and Gandhi began to eat again. This was the first time Gandhi fasted in order to change a political situation.

Harilal, Gandhi's oldest son, had met his parents in Bombay when they returned from South Africa in 1915. He travelled with them sometimes, but they still disagreed about many things. Gandhi always wanted his sons to obey him. When Harilal lost his job, his brother Manilal secretly lent him some of the *ashram's* money. When Gandhi discovered this, he sent Manilal back to South Africa to work on *Indian Opinion* at Phoenix Farm. Gandhi fasted for a few days, because of his sadness about his sons.

In June 1918, Harilal's wife and one of his children became seriously ill, and died. Harilal's other four children came to live in the *ashram*. Gandhi tried to persuade Harilal to come and live with them too, but he refused. Father and son could not understand each other.

7 The great trial (1919–1922)

The First World War was over. But in March 1919, the British government introduced a law in India which allowed them to imprison people without trial. Gandhi was extremely angry about these laws. He travelled to Delhi and then to Madras to talk to other leaders about fighting against them. In Madras he stayed with Chakravati Rajagopalachari, a lawyer who had sent money to Gandhi in South Africa and who wanted to work with him.

Gandhi's idea was that the whole of India should stop working for one day. During that day, everyone would fast and pray. Some Indian leaders were already in prison, but others joined Gandhi. The writer and Congress leader Sarojini Naidu, who had met Gandhi in London in 1914, joined the fight against the laws. She had described Gandhi in 1917 as a 'dreamer of impossible dreams . . . a strange man with . . . a calm, gentle smile'.

Across the whole of India, rich and poor, Hindus and Muslims listened to Gandhi. On 6 April, everyone stopped working. In Bombay, Gandhi spoke to a crowd of 5,000 Muslims before they went to pray. Vallabhbhai Patel helped, and Jawaharlal Nehru joined the strike in Allahabad.

There was some violence in Delhi and in Ahmedabad. In Amritsar, in the Punjab province in the far north of India, three British bankers were killed by an angry crowd after the government had arrested two leaders. Then, on 13 April 1919,

a crowd of 20,000 people went to a meeting in Jallianwala Bagh, a garden with tall buildings on every side. A new British officer, General Dyer, was commanding the soldiers in Amritsar. He had said that no meetings were allowed, but many people in the crowd did not know about this order.

General Dyer took soldiers to Jallianwala Bagh and, without warning, he ordered them to shoot. There was no escape for the crowd because the soldiers stood at the only exit. Probably more than 1,000 people were killed and more than 1,000 were injured.

People all over the world heard about this terrible crime. Many British people were ashamed of the Amritsar murders, but others collected money for General Dyer, who became ill and left India.

The memorial at Jallianwala Bagh

After this, Gandhi wanted the end of British government in India, but he was ashamed of the violence of the crowds too. He believed that the strike had been a mistake because people were not ready for *satyagraha*. He needed more people who were trained to control the crowds. He began to teach people about *satyagraha* by writing for two newspapers, *Young India* (in English) and *Navajivan* (in Gujarati).

In October 1919, the government allowed Gandhi to visit the Punjab for the first time. Many leaders were in prison,

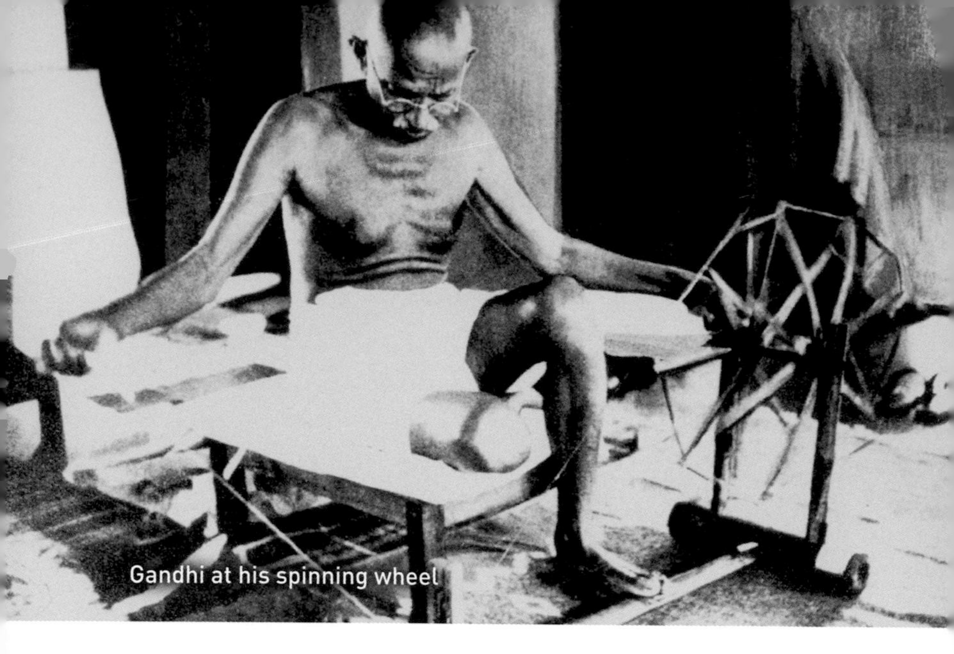
Gandhi at his spinning wheel

but Motilal Nehru and Charles Andrews came to meet him in Lahore. A great crowd met him at the railway station, and for three months he travelled through the province, talking to people about the political situation, and about the spinning wheel and the material called *khadi*.

Gandhi wanted poor villagers to be able to make their own clothes cheaply. He learnt to spin in 1917 and began to make cotton material for his own clothes. Gandhi loved his spinning wheel and used it every day for the rest of his life. The cotton from the spinning wheel was called *khadi* and it was thicker and rougher than factory cotton. More and more people began wearing clothes made of *khadi*.

Gandhi did not like the way that factories and machines had changed the lives of villagers and taken away their jobs. He wanted rich and poor people to become closer. He believed that rich people should work like everyone else and use their money, land, and factories to help other people.

Gandhi continued to travel to many cities and villages, speaking to great crowds about Muslims and Hindus working together, about changing Indian life, about spinning, and about Untouchables. When Gandhi's train was going through a town, crowds came from the towns and villages to see him. Gandhi was patient with the crowds, but at times they made it difficult for him to sleep or rest.

In 1920, Gandhi and other leaders told the Indian people that they should stop working with the British. It was time for India to have its own government. Lawyers stopped working in the courts, bankers left their jobs, and people stopped paying taxes. Nehru, Mahadev Desai, and Rajagopalachari were all sent to prison. The brothers Muhammad and Shaukat Ali, who had first met Gandhi in 1915, and Abdul Kalam Azad, a Muslim writer and Congress leader from Calcutta, were all sent to prison. By January 1922 there were about 30,000 Indians in prison.

Gandhi decided that he would not speak on Mondays. He was working very hard to change India, but he needed some private time. He kept this habit of silent Mondays until the end of his life. 'Perfect truth is in silence alone,' he wrote. He also decided to shorten his *dhoti*. Because *khadi* was more expensive than factory cloth, a shorter *dhoti* would be cheaper for poor people to wear.

Gandhi wanted all Indians to stop wearing clothes that were not made in India. In August 1921, Gandhi began to ask people to burn foreign material and clothes. Tagore (and Andrews) disagreed with Gandhi about this. Gandhi told Tagore that the poor needed work, and he continued his campaign.

In February 1922, there was violence in several cities and in Chauri Chaura, in Uttar Pradesh, an angry crowd killed a group of police. Gandhi felt responsible. He collected a team to work on a new teaching programme, called the Constructive Programme. Workers were sent to schools, to ask them to accept Untouchable children. They took spinning

Yeravda Prison

wheels to homes and talked to villagers about Hindus and Muslims working together.

In March 1922, police arrived at the *ashram* and arrested Gandhi because he was writing against the government. He was taken to the nearby Sabarmati Prison, and a week later he was taken to court. He used the trial to explain his ideas.

Gandhi agreed that he had some responsibility for the violence in the country. He told the court that he wanted to avoid violence: non-violence was his first belief, and also his last belief. 'I know that my people have sometimes gone mad. I am deeply sorry for it,' he said. But the British government had harmed India and so he chose to work against it. He spoke of the laws which sent Indians to prison without trial, and about the crime at Amritsar. India had become poorer and more helpless because of the British government, Gandhi said.

Judge Broomfield said that Gandhi was different from any other person who had ever been in his court. He realized that Gandhi had always spoken against violence, but it was his job to judge Gandhi by the law. The judge sent Gandhi to prison for six years.

At midnight, Gandhi was taken from Sabarmati Prison. He was put on a special train and taken 1,300 kilometres away, to Yeravda Prison in Poona, south of Bombay. He took with him his spinning wheel and his holy books. Gandhi was happy to go to prison, because it was part of the fight against the British government: the more Indians in prison, the more difficult it was for the British government to control India.

At Yeravda Prison, Gandhi was locked in his room alone, and allowed to walk outside for only a short time each day. He was allowed to write one letter every three months. He could borrow books from the prison library, and he read for six hours each day. He used his spinning wheel for four hours each day.

But in January 1924, after nearly two years in prison, Gandhi became seriously ill, and was quickly taken to the hospital in Poona. Gandhi was so ill that he had to stay in hospital for two months and the government decided to release him.

Leaving prison

8 The salt march (1924–1931)

When Gandhi came out of hospital, he went to stay at a friend's house on the beach in Juhu, near Bombay. He prepared himself to change his life again. He decided that he would not work against the British government until 1928, when his time in prison was meant to end. Until then, he would work for peace between groups in India, and continue his work to help poor people.

Muslims and Hindus had stopped working together, and there were arguments in Congress. At a meeting in Ahmedabad in June 1924, Gandhi cried when he realized that many people at the meeting did not agree with non-violence. Some Hindus believed that they could not work with other faiths and that violence was acceptable.

In September 1924 there was violence between Hindus and Muslims in northern India. Gandhi was staying in Delhi at the house of Muhammad Ali, his old Muslim friend. He felt helpless and hurt and he decided to fast for twenty-one days, for peace between Hindus and Muslims. He drank only water, and at first continued to write letters and to write for his newspaper.

No meat was cooked in the house while Gandhi fasted. Charles Andrews came to look after Gandhi as he became weaker. Jawaharlal Nehru was worried about him and came to visit him. They were becoming close friends, and Gandhi began to want Nehru to become India's next great leader.

Many other friends visited him: Motilal Nehru, Vinoba Bhave, Abdul Kalam Azad, and Rajagopalachari.

After twenty-one days, Gandhi was very weak. He called everyone together and asked them to be ready to die for peace between Hindus and Muslims. Gandhi asked for prayers and songs, before he began to eat again.

But the fast did not stop disagreement between Muslims and Hindus, and the violence continued. Although some Muslims continued to follow Gandhi, many no longer wanted to follow him because he was a Hindu.

Gandhi travelled again all over the country, talking to the crowds who came to see him about the Untouchables and about *khadi*. Sometimes there were crowds of 200,000 people and his voice, which was not strong, could not reach them all. So he sat in silence, and the crowd sat in silence with him.

Gandhi visited Bardoli, in southern Gujarat, and asked Vallabhbhai Patel and a group of followers to stay and work with the Untouchables and teach the villagers spinning. In 1928, the farmers in Bardoli were told that they must pay higher taxes. They asked Gandhi to help them to fight these taxes, and Vallabhbhai Patel led the fight. The villagers refused to pay the taxes and the government began to take

Talking to Untouchables

land and cows from the villagers instead of the tax. Many villagers were arrested, but there was no violence.

Gandhi called another one-day strike, and all over India people stopped working. A few days later, the government stopped the new tax. Prisoners were sent home, and land and animals were returned to the villagers.

The news that non-violence had beaten the government was reported all over India. But there were many who still used violence to fight the British government. For example, Bhagat Singh killed a police officer in Lahore in 1928 and in April 1929 he threw a bomb at a meeting in Delhi.

Gandhi and his sons sometimes disagreed. For many years he had refused to allow his sons to marry. Harilal had married without his father's agreement, but the other three sons had obeyed Gandhi. Finally, in 1927, Manilal was allowed to marry at the age of thirty-four, and Ramdas married a few months later. Devadas, who was twenty-seven, wanted to marry Rajagopalachari's daughter Lakshmi. The parents told Devadas to wait for five years, because Lakshmi was very young.

In 1928, Maganlal Gandhi died suddenly, at the age of forty-six. Maganlal had been with Gandhi in South Africa and had worked closely with Gandhi in the *ashram*. Gandhi was filled with sadness. 'He was my hands, my feet and my eyes . . . one who was dearer to me than my own sons, who never once . . . failed me,' he wrote. Many people called Gandhi *Bapu* (which means father) and Gandhi's sons knew that their father loved many people outside the family. But it must have been difficult to know that Gandhi loved Maganlal, his cousin's son, more than his own sons.

In 1930 Gandhi wrote to the Viceroy, the chief of the British government in India, explaining that he was planning another *satyagraha*. He aimed to change the ideas of the British people through non-violence: 'I do not want to hurt your people,' he wrote. He described the problems of the poor villagers, and mentioned the salt tax. No one could make or sell salt without paying a tax to the British government, and because salt was used to keep food fresh, as well as for cooking, the tax was especially difficult for poor villagers. Gandhi wanted to meet the Viceroy to discuss his letter, but the Viceroy did not reply.

On 5 March, from the *ashram*, Gandhi said that he was going to fight the salt tax. Vallabhbhai Patel, Jawaharlal Nehru, and his other friends were surprised, and at first disagreed with his plan, because the tax did not seem a serious matter. A British newspaper wrote that it was difficult not to laugh at Gandhi.

On 12 March 1930, at 6.30 a.m., Gandhi led seventy-eight people from the *ashram* and began to march south. The march had been kept secret. It was well organized and the route had been carefully planned: just over 380 kilometres, south through villages to the sea at Dandi, which had been chosen because the sea always left salt on the beach there. Some students went ahead to organize food and sleeping places. All the marchers wore *khadi*. At sixty-one years old, Gandhi was the oldest marcher.

They marched about 20 kilometres each day, and stopped at villages where Gandhi spoke to the villagers about *khadi*, and the need for Hindus to work with the Untouchables and with Muslims. Crowds came to see Gandhi and more and more people joined the march. Manilal, who was visiting from South Africa, joined the march, with Ramdas and Devadas. Every day, Gandhi wrote for the newspapers, and spent some time spinning.

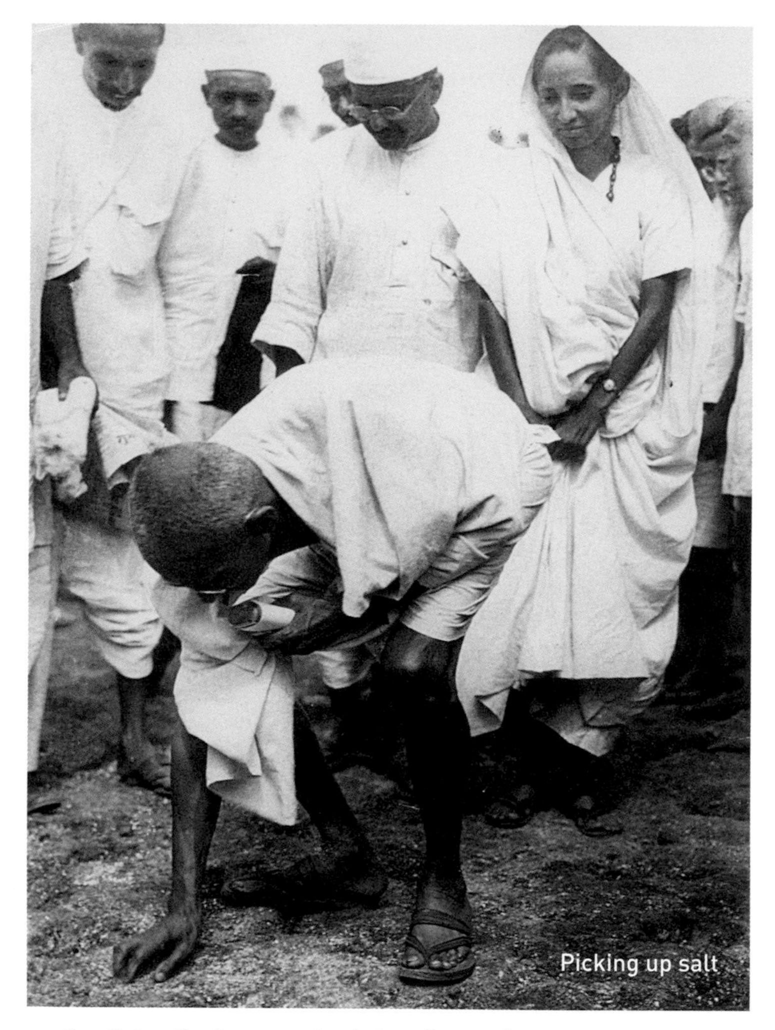

Picking up salt

On 5 April, they reached Dandi. In the morning, Gandhi went into the sea, and then picked up a handful of salt and showed it to the crowd.

And the nation followed. Now the march against the salt tax seemed a clever idea. In one town, 20,000 people went to the beach at night and collected salt. Chakravarti Rajagopalachari marched 230 kilometres, with 100 people, to collect salt from the beach in Vedaranyam. Salt was made and sold everywhere without tax.

The British government began arresting people. Jawaharlal Nehru and Rajagopalachari were put in prison. Ramdas and Devadas Gandhi were also arrested. The police beat the crowds, but there was no violence from the crowds in return.

Gandhi was still living near Dandi, sleeping outside with the other marchers. In a letter to the Viceroy, he warned that if the salt tax was not stopped, he would march to the salt works at Dharasana, 40 kilometres from Dandi. At midnight on 4 May, thirty policemen with guns came to arrest Gandhi. He was taken by train to Bombay, and then driven to prison in Poona.

But the march went ahead. Sarojini Naidu, with Manilal Gandhi and Pyarelal Nayar (Gandhi's secretary, who had joined Gandhi during his visit to the Punjab in 1919), led 2,500 marchers from Dandi to the salt works at Dharasana.

Police and soldiers were guarding the salt works. The marchers tried to go into the works, but they were beaten with sticks by the police until they fell, bleeding, to the ground. Some of them were seriously injured, but none of the marchers lifted a hand against the police.

News of the march and of the violence of the police was sent to newspapers all over the world, and the British government became unpopular with other countries. Sarojini Naidu and Manilal were arrested. About 90,000 Indians were arrested during 1930, and the British government realized that it could not continue to keep so many people in prison.

At the end of 1931, Gandhi and other leaders were released and asked to come to talk to the Viceroy in Delhi. Gandhi,

Arriving in England

Nehru, Patel, and other Congress leaders stayed with Dr Ansari, a Muslim Congress leader. Every day, Gandhi walked 8 kilometres to meet the Viceroy in his beautiful new palace, a large and extremely expensive building. Every day, after the meeting, he walked back to talk with the other leaders.

After two weeks, agreement was reached. Prisoners were sent home, and people were allowed to collect salt, though the tax remained. And Gandhi, with other leaders, was invited to London to talk to the British government.

On 29 August 1931, Gandhi sailed from Bombay with a small team: his son Devadas, Sarojini Naidu, his secretaries Mahadev Desai and Pyarelal Nayar, and Mira Slade (a British woman who had joined the *ashram* in 1925 and who had become one of Gandhi's closest helpers). While he was in London Gandhi met the film actor Charlie Chaplin, the writer George Bernard Shaw, and many other famous people. He had tea with King George the Fifth, and he spoke at a vegetarian meeting.

Gandhi did not stay in a famous hotel, but in a poor house in the East End of London where he slept on the floor. He walked through the streets and children followed him. He travelled to the north of England to meet factory workers who had lost jobs because of Gandhi's work against foreign textiles.

Newspapers were interested in everything about Gandhi, and he became popular with many British people. But the meetings about India's future were not successful. To the British government, Gandhi was only one of many Indian leaders who did not agree with each other. Gandhi wanted all Indians to work together to make the British leave India. But Muslim leaders wanted a separate assembly, and Dr Ambedkar, the leader of the Untouchables, also wanted a separate assembly. They did not want Gandhi to speak for them.

The British were not leaving India yet.

Gandhi with English factory workers

9 'A message to all India' (1932–1939)

Gandhi arrived in Bombay at the end of December 1931. Kasturba, Patel, and Rajagopalachari were there to meet him and tell him that Jawaharlal Nehru and several Muslim leaders had just been arrested. The situation had changed. There was a new government in Britain, and a new Viceroy, Lord Willingdon, in India.

That evening, Gandhi spoke to a crowd of 200,000. He was ready to continue the fight of non-violence against the government. He sent a message to the new Viceroy, but Willingdon refused to meet him. On 4 January 1932, Gandhi was arrested.

Once again, Gandhi said goodbye to Kasturba. Once again, there was no trial. Gandhi was driven to Yeravda Prison in Poona. This time, the guards wanted to give Gandhi furniture and special food, but he refused. Vallabhbhai Patel and Mahadev Desai were in prison with him, and they were allowed to meet. Patel was always able to make them laugh, but Gandhi was worried about Kasturba and Devadas who had also been sent to prison.

In August, the British government decided to give the Untouchables a separate assembly. Gandhi had already decided that if this happened, he would fast to death. Gandhi believed strongly that the Untouchables should be accepted by everyone, not kept separate, and he wanted Dr Ambedkar to change his mind about the separate assembly.

Gandhi wrote to Tagore and to the Indian leaders to explain the reasons for the fast, and news about the fast appeared in the newspapers.

The weather was very hot. Gandhi lay on a bed outside, under a tree. He drank only water, and became weak very quickly. After a few days, Kasturba was moved from Sabarmati Prison to Yeravda to be with Gandhi during the fast. She shook her head when she saw him. 'Again, the same story!' she said. Gandhi smiled.

Sarojini Naidu was brought from the women's prison to help look after Gandhi. Patel and Desai sat near him. Tagore was allowed to visit him, and he sang some of his songs to Gandhi, who was too weak to speak. Tagore said that Gandhi's fast was 'a message to all India and to the world. Let us try to understand what the message means.'

Jawaharlal Nehru was in prison and at first he did not agree with the fast. But all over India, places were opened to Untouchables. In many cities, Hindus invited Untouchables to eat with them. When Nehru heard about the changes in the country, he began to understand.

But Dr Ambedkar disagreed with the fast. His people had suffered terribly for centuries at the hands of the Hindus, but he came to see Gandhi in prison. Rajagopalachari negotiated with Ambedkar, who finally agreed to one assembly, with some seats kept for Untouchables.

Tagore was with Gandhi when his fast ended, on 26 September. Gandhi was released in May 1933. The government had closed *Young India*, so Gandhi started a new newspaper which he called *Harijan*. *Harijan*, which means 'children of God' was the name he gave to the Untouchables. (This name, like Untouchables, is now unacceptable.)

For ten months, Gandhi travelled all over India, this time

speaking only about the Untouchables. Wherever he went, he had meetings with them and collected money for them. This was the fifth time he had travelled all over the country. Some people did not agree with his beliefs. In Bihar province, a crowd beat his car with sticks. And in Poona, a bomb was thrown at Gandhi's car, although he was not in it.

The government planned to take the land from the *ashram* at Sabarmati because Gandhi had refused to pay tax, and so Gandhi decided to close the *ashram*. He was given land for a new *ashram* in Sevagram, near Wardha, a small town in the centre of India. Many orange trees grew there, and it was extremely hot. In the 1920s, Gandhi had sent Vinoba Bhave to Wardha to start an *ashram*. (Gandhi once said that Vinoba Bhave understood his message better than Gandhi did himself.) Most of the villagers in Sevagram were Untouchables, and Gandhi began to teach them how to spin.

In 1934, Gandhi decided to leave Congress to give younger leaders the chance to lead. Indians were now involved in the government of India, and in 1937 there were elections. It was clear that Muslims were not voting for Congress.

Muhammad Ali Jinnah

The Muslim League, led by Muhammad Ali Jinnah, was popular in some parts of India. Jinnah had studied law in London. He had belonged to Congress but left in 1920. He was rich, and lived in a large house in Bombay. He did not like

Gandhi's beliefs about changing the lives of Indians. He believed that Congress was a Hindu group and Gandhi a Hindu leader, and that the Muslim League was the only group for Muslims.

Gandhi walking with Ghaffar Khan

Jinnah now wanted a separate Muslim nation. Gandhi thought that talk of two nations was unhelpful and irresponsible: each part of India consisted of different groups who had lived together for centuries.

Gandhi did have some strong Muslim followers. Ghaffar Khan was a Congress leader who believed in non-violence. He was born in 1890 in the mountains in the north-west of India, near the Khyber Pass. He and his brother began to follow Gandhi's ideas in 1919, when he organized Gandhi's strike in his village, Utmanzai, near Peshawar. His family was rich, but he lived like a poor man, and he was sent to prison many times by the British.

The government had refused to allow Gandhi to visit the north-west for a long time, but in 1938 he was allowed to visit twice, and in 1939 he went again with Kasturba. Ghaffar Khan was his guide as he visited many villages. He spoke to the crowds about non-violence, about *khadi* and about the need to change women's lives. And of course he spoke about his dream: that Muslims and Hindus would live and work together peacefully. The two men looked very different: Ghaffar Khan was tall and thin, with a beard, and Gandhi was very small. But their beliefs were the same.

Kasturba was arrested in Rajkot in 1939, and Gandhi wrote to her every day. Finally, he went to Rajkot himself and fasted until she was allowed to leave prison.

The Second World War was coming and Gandhi was asked many times about his opinion of Hitler, who had been voted into government in Germany. Gandhi's belief in non-violence was stronger than before. He thought that the horror of this war would be greater than the First World War, but he did not believe in any war. Hitler was responsible for the war, he wrote, and Germans should refuse to obey him.

Many visitors from all over the world came to see Gandhi at Sevagram *ashram*. His old friend Hermann Kallenbach visited him from South Africa for two months at the beginning of 1939. Gandhi understood the anger that Kallenbach, himself a Jew, felt about the suffering of Jews in Germany. African Americans also visited Gandhi and talked to him about their situation and their future. The African American leaders Marcus Garvey and W. E. B. Du Bois often spoke and wrote about Gandhi.

Gandhi continued to wake up early every day. He wrote letters, ate little, and walked every day, usually with the women of the *ashram*. He enjoyed talking to his companions and to visitors, and he loved playing with the children of the *ashram*.

If anyone became ill, *Bapu* would help to care for them. For years, he looked after a man with leprosy, a terrible disease which most people feared.

Visitors noticed his frequent laughter, but they also noticed his sadness. The violence of the war was painful to Gandhi. He argued with God 'in the secret of [his] heart', he wrote, because God allowed these terrible things to happen. But he would go on without losing faith in God.

10 Prison (1939–1944)

Britain took India into the war against Germany in September 1939. Indian leaders met the Viceroy. Gandhi wanted to give Britain peaceful help during the war, and Jinnah wanted to help Britain if Muslims were helped. But Nehru and other younger leaders would not agree to help Britain unless freedom was promised.

Gandhi travelled to Calcutta in 1940 to visit Charles Andrews, who was seriously ill. Andrews, who lived in Tagore's school, died a few months later. He was the last person who called Gandhi by his name 'Mohandas'. They had met as brothers in South Africa and had remained brothers to the end. It was also Gandhi's last meeting with Tagore, who died in 1941.

The Muslim League was becoming more and more popular with Muslims, and therefore Jinnah was becoming stronger. In 1940, the Muslim League agreed with Jinnah that it wanted a Muslim nation, separate from India. The Congress leader Abul Kalam Azad, who was proud to be an Indian Muslim, did not want India to become two nations. He really wanted to talk to Jinnah, but Jinnah refused to meet with him.

Many Indians began to disobey the British government again. Gandhi asked Vinoba Bhave to lead this *satyagraha*. Nehru, Patel, Azad, and other Congress leaders were arrested, and soon about 15,000 Indians were in prison. But they were released in December 1941.

In 1941, America joined the war against Hitler. The

Japanese army was fighting the British in China, and it was possible that the Japanese army would land in India.

In August 1942, Gandhi spoke at a Congress meeting in Bombay. He told Congress that the British must leave India, and that all Indians should behave like free men and women. 'We shall either free India, or die in the attempt,' he said. Gandhi spoke for a long time and then he returned to Birla House where he was staying with Kasturba, Mahadev Desai, and Pyarelal Nayar.

Mahadev Desai reads a letter from the Viceroy

That night, the police came to arrest Gandhi and other Congress leaders. Gandhi and Desai were taken by train to Poona. Then they were taken across the River Mula to the grand Aga Khan Palace, with its large gardens, which the British had taken to use during the war.

Nehru, Patel, Azad, and nine other Congress leaders were taken to Ahnednagar, a sixteenth century castle. They were able to meet and talk together while in prison there. Some of them agreed with Gandhi's 'leave India' idea, but Azad and others disagreed.

Kasturba was arrested and taken to join Gandhi's group in prison. Mahadev Desai and Sarojini Naidu were with him, as well as Mira Slade, Dr Sushila Nayar (Pyarelal's sister who had joined Gandhi in 1939), and Manu Gandhi (who came to live with her great-uncle in 1942, when she was fourteen, to help Kasturba).

A few days after arriving at the Aga Khan Palace, Mahadev Desai died suddenly, aged 50. Desai had been Gandhi's secretary since 1917. He had worked closely with Gandhi and travelled with him all over India. Gandhi called Mahadev his son, and Kasturba said that Desai was Gandhi's left hand and his right hand. Twice a day while he was in prison, Gandhi took flowers to the place where Desai's ashes were buried.

There was violence in many parts of India after the arrests. Police stations were burnt down, police were killed, and bombs were thrown at bridges. The police killed more than 1,000 people.

The Viceroy blamed Gandhi for the violence, and Gandhi decided to fast for twenty-one days, in February 1943, to prove that he wanted peace. Two doctors were allowed to look after Gandhi, who became seriously ill during the fast. Kasturba and the doctors thought that he was going to die. But, after the fast, very slowly he became stronger.

Kasturba was ill when she was sent to prison, and in December 1943 she became seriously ill. Her sons were allowed to visit her, and doctors looked after her. In February 1944 Kasturba died in her husband's arms.

Her death was terribly painful for Gandhi. Their marriage was unusual, because since 1906 they had lived not as husband and wife but as part of an *ashram*. Kasturba did not always agree with Gandhi and he was sometimes angry with her. But although she could read and write only a little, he learned a lot from her. They had been married for sixty-two years; they cared deeply for each other and always wanted to be together.

After Kasturba's death, Gandhi became ill and his friends and doctors were worried about him. The government did not want him to die in prison and so they released him in April 1944.

He went first to the house at Juhu, where he had stayed in 1924. Then he stayed for a few weeks in a town in the hills, south of Poona. Rajagopalachari was there, too, and Gandhi was happy to be with his old friend. Slowly, Gandhi became stronger and in August he returned to Sevagram *ashram*.

Gandhi with his son Devdas after Kasturba's death

11 Working for peace (1944–1946)

In September 1944, Gandhi was in Bombay, staying at Birla House. Ghanshyam Das Birla was a very rich factory owner who first met Gandhi in Calcutta in 1915. He did not always agree with Gandhi, but he regularly gave money to Gandhi's *ashrams* and other programmes. Birla had houses in Delhi and Bombay, and Gandhi had stayed with him several times.

Jinnah's house was on the same road, and Gandhi walked there to talk to him about the situation in India. Jinnah was seriously ill, but they met every day for two weeks. Jinnah wanted a separate Muslim state, Pakistan, before the British left India. Gandhi wanted to wait until India was free and he did not want the new nation to be completely separate from India. Jinnah and Gandhi could not reach an agreement.

Gandhi with Jinnah

In 1945, the Second World War ended and Nehru and the other leaders were allowed to leave Ahmednagar Prison.

There was a new Viceroy, and he called all the leaders to a meeting to talk about India's future. Gandhi travelled third-class by train, in the summer heat, to Simla, the government's summer capital. Simla was in the hills, with views of the snow-covered Himalaya mountains.

Gandhi, now seventy-five years old, felt tired and sad, and he wanted the younger leaders to have control. But the meeting in Simla failed. Jinnah would not accept the Muslim Congress leaders and he even refused to shake Azad's hand. He wanted the Muslim League to have control of all Muslim votes, and he asked all Muslims to work for Pakistan.

There was a new British government which promised that Britain would leave India. In March 1946 the British government sent a team to India to plan for an Indian government and to solve the Pakistan problem. The Viceroy asked Gandhi to come to Delhi to meet the team.

As the Congress leaders negotiated with the British, Gandhi was still involved. But at one meeting, Gandhi advised the Congress leaders not to accept the ideas of the British. There was a long silence and no one spoke. Finally, Gandhi got up and left the meeting.

The British agreed to a new Indian government, and Jawaharlal Nehru became head of this government. India would become completely independent in 1947.

There had been violence in Calcutta in August 1946, and many Hindus and Muslims were killed. And in September, there was violence in Bombay, and in the provinces of Punjab, Bengal, and Bihar. Most violence was in the cities, but in October, there was violence in the villages of Noakhali, in East Bengal, where Muslims killed Hindus. Then, in revenge, Hindus killed Muslims in Bihar.

Nehru flew to Bihar to talk to the people there. Gandhi

Laughing with Nehru

decided to go to Noakhali. He went first by train to Calcutta. As he drove through the city with Hasan Shaheed Suhrawardy, the leader of Bengal, Gandhi saw the burned houses and destroyed shops, with rubbish everywhere on the streets. Suhrawardy belonged to the Muslim League, but he had known Gandhi for years and called him *Bapu*.

Gandhi left for Noakhali with a group of companions on 6 November. He was going as God's servant, he said. He was saddened by the pain of others, by 'the madness that can turn a man into less than an animal'. He believed that he was partly responsible for the violence: he had probably made mistakes and he blamed himself, and so he had to work to change the situation. He did not know what he would be able to do in Noakhali, but he knew that he had to go there to be at peace with himself.

Gandhi went by train and then by ship to Chaumuhani, a land of rivers and trees, where Muslims and Hindus had lived together for centuries.

For four months, Gandhi went from village to village, travelling by boat or on foot. The weather was cold. In each village he stayed in the house of a poor farmer, often a Muslim, and sat outside to pray and listen to the villagers. Every day he read from the *Qur'an*, did his spinning, and wrote letters. Usually he slept for only four hours each night. Manu cooked for him, and Professor Nirmal Bose, from Calcutta, also went with him and began to teach him to speak Bengali.

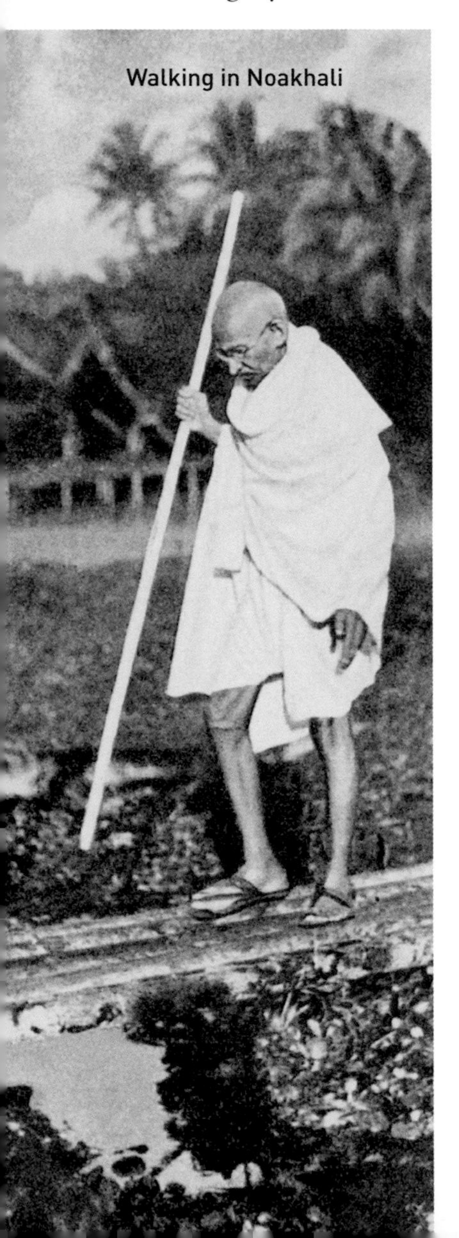

Walking in Noakhali

The others in his team – Pyarelal and his sister Sushila, Kanu Gandhi and his young wife Abha – were all sent separately to different villages to teach about peace. It was dangerous for all of them. Gandhi knew he could be killed and he was ready to die. But, in all the villages they stayed in, their work resulted in peace.

In those four months, Gandhi visited forty-nine villages. Hindus met him with songs, and Muslims were usually friendly, although some did not like him to read from the *Qur'an*. In every village, he asked the villagers to promise not to murder others again. He visited women and sick children, and met Untouchables. He often walked without shoes. His feet were covered with cuts, and he had to walk carefully over narrow wooden bridges.

He often sang one of Tagore's songs, 'Walk alone', and he repeated the words from the Christian song that he had loved since his days in South Africa: 'one step enough for me'.

Some Indian leaders continued to ask Gandhi for advice while he was in Noakhali. In December, Nehru travelled from Delhi to tell him about the recent meetings in London about Pakistan.

In March 1947, Gandhi left Noakhali and travelled to Bihar. Bihar was special to Gandhi because it was the province where he had worked to help the indigo farmers in 1917. The Hindus in Bihar had wanted revenge for the violence in neighbouring Noakhali: in November 1946, crowds had killed about 7,000 Muslims.

Although it was four months since the violence, Muslims in Bihar were still afraid. Gandhi immediately began to visit towns and villages. He visited Muslim families and listened to them, and he asked Hindus to help Muslims return to their homes. Many Hindus gave money to help Muslims to rebuild their lives. Ghaffar Khan came to join Gandhi, and helped with his work there.

Gandhi was now seventy-seven years old, and he said that he would not rest, nor let others rest: there was a fire burning in him, and he could have no peace until he could solve the problem of the violence.

12 'My life is my message' (1947–1948)

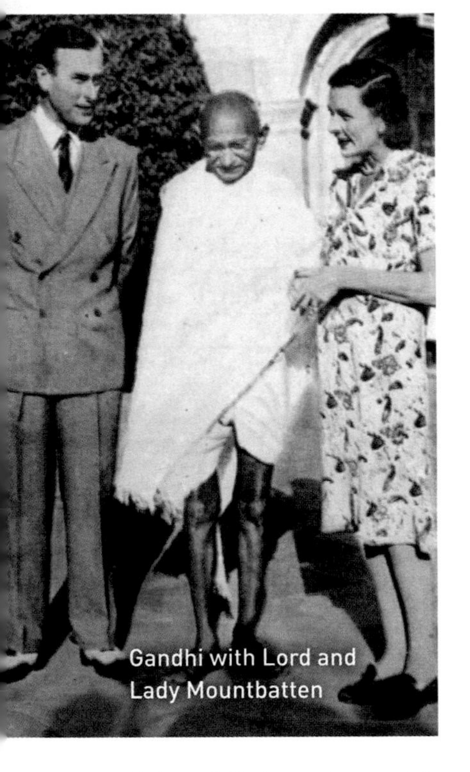

Gandhi with Lord and Lady Mountbatten

In March 1947, the last Viceroy of India, Lord Mountbatten, arrived in Delhi and immediately began meeting Indian leaders. He invited Gandhi to come and see him, and Gandhi travelled 800 kilometres by train from Bihar.

Gandhi met the Viceroy several times, and Jinnah also met Lord Mountbatten. Gandhi met Nehru and the other Congress leaders, but they did not accept his ideas for a peaceful answer to the question of Pakistan. Among other ideas, he suggested that Jinnah should become the new Prime Minister. But neither Mountbatten nor the Congress leaders liked this idea.

So he went back to Bihar to continue his work there. Twice in May he was called back to Delhi. He also went to Calcutta, to meet with leaders there. Bengal was going to be divided, and he tried to stop this.

Walking in Bihar with Ghaffar Khan

But he did not succeed. The Punjab in the west and Bengal in the east were divided, part to remain in India, and part to become the new nation, Pakistan. Congress voted to accept Pakistan.

Gandhi felt alone. Only Ghaffar Khan and his brother agreed with him. His heart burned with pain. The nation was not with Gandhi, and he disagreed with what his friends were doing. And other Hindus were angry with him because he could not prevent India from being divided.

Gandhi travelled to Calcutta at the beginning of August. He did not want to be in Delhi when Pakistan became a nation on 14 August 1947 and India became independent on 15 August. He planned to go to Noakhali, which would be in Pakistan, because the people there were afraid of more violence. But when Gandhi reached Calcutta, Hasan Shaheed Suhrawardy asked him to stay because Muslims in Calcutta were afraid. Gandhi agreed, if Suhrawardy would live with him.

They moved to an old Muslim house, and together they spoke to all visitors. Together, they met Hindus in the poor parts of the city. On 15 August, while Jawaharlal Nehru, the leader of the newly independent India, spoke to the world in Delhi, Gandhi stayed quietly in the house in Calcutta. He wrote letters and prayed with a crowd of Hindus and Muslims. Abha and Manu Gandhi were with him.

Late at night on 31 August, an angry crowd of Hindus broke the windows of the house in Calcutta. Gandhi opened his door, and a stone and a stick were thrown at him. Police were able to move the crowd away, and no one in the house was injured. But in the morning, Gandhi heard that people had been killed in the streets.

Gandhi decided to stay in Calcutta and fast until peace returned to the city. News of his fast immediately changed the situation. Groups of Hindus and Muslims brought their weapons to Gandhi and promised to stop the violence, and Hindus and Muslims walked together through the city. Young people started a peace group to work for peace in the city. They asked Gandhi for a message, and he wrote a few words for them: 'My life is my message'.

On the evening of 4 September, when there had been no violence in Calcutta for twenty-four hours, Suhrawardy came to Gandhi with leaders of all the groups in Calcutta. They asked Gandhi to end his fast. He told them that they must promise to give their lives to prevent violence. And they promised.

Gandhi had fasted for seventy-three hours, and peace had come to Calcutta. But the violence in the Punjab was worsening, and Gandhi offered to go there to help. On 7 September, Gandhi left Calcutta. He went by train first to Delhi, a journey of two days.

Vallabhbhai Patel met him at the station. Violence had started in Delhi and many people had been killed. Gandhi would have to stay at Birla House, in the rich part of the city, because his usual place would not be safe. This was another sadness for Gandhi.

Crowds of Hindus and Sikhs had left the Punjab to escape from the violence there. By the middle of 1948, about 5,500,000 Hindus and Sikhs had left their homes in Pakistan and arrived in India without money. The same number of Muslims left their homes in India and went to Pakistan.

Gandhi went immediately to visit the refugees in Delhi. They told him about their fear and about the violence they had suffered. Many Hindus in Delhi wanted to get rid of all the Muslims in the city. Gandhi realized that there was work for him to do in Delhi, and so he decided to stay. Delhi was the capital of India: if there was violence in Delhi, there could be no peace in the rest of India.

Gandhi met M. S. Golwalkar, the chief of the extreme Hindu group Rashtriya Swayamsevak Sangh (RSS). This group, started in 1925, believed that Hindus should live separately from Muslims and Untouchables. The group trained young Hindus to use sticks and knives. Gandhi wanted the RSS leaders to prevent their followers from using violence against Muslims.

Gandhi lived his usual simple life in Birla House. He sat on the floor to spin, to eat, and to talk to visitors. He slept outside, with his companions nearby. Every day he walked through the garden for a prayer meeting, which was open to everyone. He spoke to the small crowd, and always read some words from the *Qur'an*.

More and more refugees came to Delhi from Pakistan. The violence in Delhi itself continued. Every day Gandhi went

Gandhi at Birla House

across the city, listening to the sad stories of the refugees, meeting with Muslim leaders, talking to crowds. He visited injured Muslims in hospital and tried to persuade them not to leave their homes, but they were afraid to stay.

It was Gandhi's seventy-eighth birthday on 2 October 1947. Messages came from all over the world and many visitors came to see him: Nehru, Patel, Birla. But Gandhi's heart was full of pain. He felt helpless and he asked his visitors to pray that God would take him away: he did not want another birthday with India still in flames.

Nehru and Patel, leaders of India and of Congress, often disagreed with each other and came to talk to Gandhi. They listened to him, but did not always follow his advice.

Brij Krishna, who had worked with Gandhi in Delhi since the 1920s, was living with him. Abha and Manu Gandhi were looking after him. Manu also worked as his secretary, because Pyarelal was working in Noakhali. Pyarelal came to Delhi in December 1947, and Gandhi was happy to see him and talk to him about the situation there.

On 12 January 1948, as he sat in the garden at Birla House, Gandhi decided to fast again. He had not told Nehru or the other leaders. Gandhi wanted real peace: he wanted all Hindus, Muslims, and Sikhs in India and Pakistan to live at peace with each other.

He lay on a bed outside Birla House, covered with a *khadi* blanket. Dr Sushila Nayar looked after him, and her brother Pyarelal was with him. Visitors came to see him. Abul Kalam Azad was extremely worried about Gandhi's weakness and asked him to drink, but Gandhi found this difficult.

As soon as people knew that Gandhi was fasting, the situation began to change. The Sikhs in Delhi invited a group of Muslims to return to Delhi. Peaceful crowds walked through the city and there was less violence in Pakistan. On 17 January, Gandhi sent Pyarelal to go through the city to find out if Muslims were safe yet.

Leaders of all groups met in the house of Rajendra Prasad, a lawyer from Bihar who had worked with Gandhi in Champaran in 1918, and who was now leading Congress. On the sixth day of Gandhi's fast, more than 100 leaders came from Prasad's house to Birla House. They were from all the different groups in Delhi – Sikhs, Hindus, Muslims. Nehru was there, and Azad, leaders from the RSS and from the Pakistan government. Rajendra Prasad told Gandhi that all the leaders had promised to help Muslims to return to their homes in Delhi.

In tears, Gandhi told them that he would fast again if necessary. There were prayers and songs. Nehru was in tears, as Azad gave Gandhi a glass of orange to drink.

Gandhi was thin and weak after this fast. The next day, he was carried to the evening prayer meeting.

On 20 January, as he was speaking at the evening prayer meeting, there was a loud noise nearby. The crowd was afraid, but Gandhi said to them, 'Listen! Listen! Nothing has happened.' He did not realize that a bomb had been thrown towards him from the garden wall. Mandanlal Pahwa was one of a group of young Hindus who had decided to kill Gandhi because of his views on Muslims and non-violence.

Afterwards, Gandhi was told about the bomb. The next day, he told the crowd that no one should hate the person responsible for the bomb: that person probably believed that Gandhi was an enemy of Hindus and that God wanted him to kill Gandhi.

Gandhi realized that many people hated him. He received many letters which accused him of working against Hindus. Sometimes at his meetings people shouted, 'Death to Gandhi!' Some Hindu refugees, wounded when escaping from Pakistan, told him that he should disappear, that he had done enough harm with his message of love and non-violence.

But Gandhi remained peaceful. There was no bitterness in his heart. Gandhi wanted to see Ghaffar Khan and his brother, and he began to plan his visit to Pakistan. He would continue to work for peace between all groups and to follow God.

13 Father of the Nation (1948 – and beyond)

On Friday 30 January 1948, Gandhi woke up early as usual for morning prayers. Then he worked on his new ideas for Congress. He had a meeting with the leaders of the Muslims in Delhi. Later, he met a group of Hindu refugees, and a group of Sikhs, as well as a group visiting from the Punjab. During lunch he spoke to Pyarelal about his work in Noakhali. He had decided to go to the *ashram* at Sevagram first, before going to Pakistan, and he began to plan his journey with Brij Krishna.

Then Vallabhbhai Patel arrived for a meeting with him. Gandhi did his spinning, and ate his dinner of vegetables and fruit while talking to Patel. Gandhi told Patel that he must continue to work with Nehru: India needed both of them. Gandhi said that he planned to tell Nehru the same thing when he saw him later that day.

Their conversation was longer than Gandhi expected: he was ten minutes late for prayers, and he hated to be late. He walked quickly from his room with Manu and Abha, his hands on their shoulders.

The crowd was waiting, and Gandhi went up the steps and along the path to the platform where he sat for prayers. Men and women stood and touched their hands together in the usual sign of welcome as Gandhi passed them. He replied by putting his hands together as he walked.

Suddenly, a man pushed forward into the path and bent

down, as if he wanted to touch Gandhi's feet. Manu told the man that they were hurrying because they were late. The man pushed her away. He took out a gun and shot Gandhi three times in the chest. Slowly, Gandhi fell to the ground. 'Hey Rama (oh God),' he said quietly as he fell. His white clothes quickly became stained with blood.

Brij Krishna, who had been following Gandhi, ran to help. Gently, Gandhi was carried back to his room in Birla House. A doctor was soon there, but there was nothing he could do: Gandhi was dead.

Patel was still nearby, and he sat by Gandhi's body with Gandhi's companions until Nehru arrived. Nehru knelt by Gandhi's body, and cried. Devadas, Gandhi's youngest son, soon arrived, followed by Azad and other leaders.

Patel told Nehru about Gandhi's last message to them both. Their arguments were over; they would work together until Patel died in 1950. The two men went together to speak to India on the radio.

Nehru spoke in Hindi and then in English. 'The light has gone out of our lives and there is darkness everywhere. I do not know what to tell you or how to say it. Our [dear] leader, *Bapu* as we called him, the Father of the Nation, is no more.'

All over India and Pakistan, people heard the terrible news of Gandhi's death and they were filled with sadness.

On 31 January, Gandhi's body left Birla House and was taken slowly through the large crowds to the Raj Ghat, 10 kilometres away. Gandhi's body was put on a platform of stones and wood by the holy River Yamuna, as 1,000,000 people watched. Ramdas lit the fire, and prayers were sung for fourteen hours, until only ashes were left.

Then, Gandhi's ashes were put on a special train, in a

Gandhi's funeral, 31 January 1948

third-class compartment, and taken to Allahabad, where the holy Rivers Ganges and Yamuna meet. At every station crowds waited, as they had waited for him when he was alive.

On 12 February, Gandhi's ashes were taken from the train and put in a car. Nehru walked behind the car, as it drove to the river. Azad, Patel, and Sarojini Naidu were there, as well as Gandhi's sons. The ashes were put into the river, and were taken by the river to the sea.

All over the world people were hurt by the news of Gandhi's death. Messages came from leaders and friends, and from many who had never met him. Leon Blum, a French leader, wrote: 'I never saw Gandhi. I do not speak his language. I never set foot in his country. And yet I feel the same [sadness] as if I had lost someone near and dear.'

In Pakistan, Jinnah said that Gandhi was 'one of the greatest men' of India.

The man who killed Gandhi was called Nathuram Godse. He and Mandanlal Pahwa (who had thrown the bomb near Birla House) belonged to the same group. Godse hated Gandhi's beliefs, but at his trial he said that before he shot Gandhi, he 'actually wished him well'. Manilal and Ramdas Gandhi asked the government not to kill Godse, but the government disagreed and he was put to death.

And so Gandhi's life ended in violence, but his message did not end, and many people all over the world have followed his ideas. Many of his friends and companions wrote diaries and books about him. Gandhi had written so much during his life that his words are collected into 100 books.

Martin Luther King, in the United States of America, read about Gandhi and chose the path of non-violence to fight against racism in his country.

The Dalai Lama, leader of Tibet, visited Raj Ghat when he was twenty-one years old. He wondered what advice Gandhi would have for a young leader. He felt that Gandhi told him to follow the path of peace, and he decided never to accept violence.

In South Africa, many Africans followed Gandhi's beliefs. Desmond Tutu in South Africa believes that Gandhi's path is the only one that can bring peace to the world.

The world still waits for peace, but wherever there is violence, there are also people working for peace, and Gandhi's life and message continue to help them to be strong.

Many tourists visit India. Perhaps you, too, may go there one day, and see the house in Porbandar where Mohandas Karamchand Gandhi was born. You can visit his *ashram* in

Sevagram, and the Aga Khan Palace, where he was in prison and where Kasturba's ashes are buried. Birla House is open to visitors. You can see his room there, and the place where he was murdered.

All his life, Gandhi tried to be honest and brave. He followed his beliefs as truly as he could, although that often made life difficult for him. He believed that violence was usually unsuccessful, and did not allow people to change. He knew he made mistakes, but he always tried to learn from them. When he fasted, he wanted to show God that he was hurt by something and that he was sorry; he was also trying to persuade people to change their lives.

At times, Gandhi had doubts and was filled with desperate sadness when he saw what was happening around him, but he kept his deep faith in God and his love for all people. Years after his death, Gandhi's message is still extremely important to the world.

Raj Ghat – the Gandhi memorial

GLOSSARY

ahimsa refusal to kill or harm any living thing; non-violence
ash the grey powder that is left when something has been burnt
ashram a place where a group of people live together peacefully, away from others
assembly a group of people who meet together regularly to make laws and decisions
Bhagavad Gita a holy book of the Hindu faith
belief something that is believed
campaign a plan to do a number of things in order to get a special result
Christian a person who believes in Jesus Christ
compartment part of a train where people sit
conference a meeting to discuss opinions and make plans
corps a group of people involved in a particular job
congress a political group
court a place where trials happen
divide to separate into different parts
dhoti a long piece of material, covering the legs and tied at the waist, worn by men
election a time when people choose their government by voting
empire several countries governed by another nation
faith a way of following God; a strong religious belief
fast (*n & v*) to eat little or no food for a time
force something that has a lot of power or influence
govern to have legal control of a country; (*n*) **government**
Hindu a person who follows Hinduism, the chief faith in India
holy connected with a particular religion
imprison to put somebody in prison
independent (of a country) having its own government
injustice something that is wrong and unfair
Jew a person who follows the faith of Judaism
khadi cotton material made by hand, not in a factory
leprosy a serious disease of the skin

march (*n & v*) a long organized walk
memorial something that is used to remember a person or event
miner someone who works under the ground, digging for valuable stones
Muslim someone who follows the faith of Islam
negotiate to discuss and try to reach agreement
non-violence refusal to use violence
political involved with matters of government
pray (*v*) to speak to God; (*n*) **prayer**
province a large part of a country which has some of its own government officials
Qur'an the holy book of the Muslim faith
racism belief that one group of people is better than others
refugee someone who has to leave their country because of danger
release (*v*) to let a person go free
right (*n*) the ability by law to have the chance to do something, e.g. to vote, go to school etc
satyagraha truth-force or love-force; the practice of non-violent resistance
spin (*v*) to make thread from cotton by twisting it
strike (*n*) a time when people refuse to work, in order to get what they want
suffer (*v*) to feel pain or sadness
tax money paid to the government
textile material made from thread in factories
turban a long piece of material worn round the head
vegetarian a person who does not eat meat or fish
Viceroy a person governing a country, in place of the king or queen of another country
violence use of great force in order to injure someone or damage something
vote to choose the person you want in an election

ACTIVITIES

Before Reading

1 Read the back cover, and the introduction on the first page. Are these sentences true (T) or false (F)?

1 Gandhi was born in India.
2 Gandhi fought for poor people.
3 After his death, the world forgot about Gandhi.
4 Gandhi agreed to move out of a first-class compartment on a train, because a white passenger wanted to sit in it.

2 How much do you know about Gandhi's life? Circle one word in each sentence.

1 When Gandhi was born, India was controlled by *China / Britain / South Africa*.
2 Gandhi was against *marriage / business / violence*.
3 Sometimes Gandhi worked as a *soldier / nurse / pilot*.
4 Gandhi was famous for making his own *clothes / house / food*.
5 When he was older, Gandhi always wore *expensive / black / simple* clothes.
6 Gandhi died in *1908 / 1948 / 2008*.

3 Which of these things do you think you are going to read about in the book? Why? Tick eight boxes.

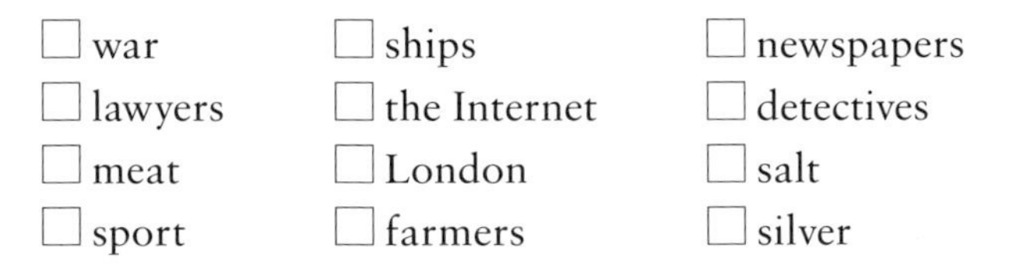
☐ war ☐ ships ☐ newspapers
☐ lawyers ☐ the Internet ☐ detectives
☐ meat ☐ London ☐ salt
☐ sport ☐ farmers ☐ silver

ACTIVITIES

While Reading

Read Chapter 1, then circle the correct words.

1 Mohandas was very *shy* / *angry* when he was a boy.
2 Mohandas was the *oldest* / *youngest* child in his family.
3 Mohandas was not allowed to eat *fish* / *meat*.
4 At *thirteen* / *twenty-three*, Mohandas married.
5 Mohandas went to London to study *science* / *law*.
6 He stayed in London for *three years* / *six months*.
7 While Mohandas was in London, his *mother* / *father* died.
8 Mohandas was offered a job in South Africa because he could speak *Spanish* / *English*.

Read Chapters 2 and 3, then rewrite these untrue sentences with the correct information.

1 Durban was a South African city in the German Empire.
2 In a courtroom in Durban, a judge told Gandhi to take off his jacket, but Gandhi refused.
3 When Gandhi was travelling to Pretoria by train, the guards asked him to move out of the third-class compartment.
4 Gandhi brought his wife and daughters to live with him in South Africa.
5 When war started in South Africa in 1899, Gandhi decided to help the Afrikaners.
6 Gandhi called together a large group of Indians to help care for pilots who were wounded during the war.

Read Chapters 4 and 5. Match these halves of sentences.

1 Gandhi started a newspaper called *Indian Opinion*, . . .
2 Gandhi met a reporter called Henry Polak . . .
3 After reading a book by John Ruskin, . . .
4 Everyone at Gandhi's farm in Phoenix . . .
5 Gandhi's son was angry . . .
6 Poor Indians called Gandhi *Mahatma*, . . .

a at a vegetarian restaurant.
b which means 'great soul'.
c Gandhi decided to live a simpler life.
d because his father refused to let him study in London.
e and he wrote for it every week.
f earned £3 each month.

Read Chapter 6, then answer these questions.

1 How was Gandhi different from other Indian leaders?
2 What kind of factories were there at Ahmedabad?
3 Why did gifts to Gandhi's *ashram* suddenly stop?
4 Which language did Gandhi usually use?
5 Before 1917, what did farmers in Champaran have to grow?
6 What did Manilal do when Harilal lost his job?

Read Chapter 7. Fill in the gaps with these words.

court, crowd, government, imprisoned, injured, judge, law, released, shoot, War, warning

1 After the First World _____, the British _____ introduced a _____ in India which allowed people to be _____ without trial.
2 There was a large _____ in a garden in Amritsar.

Without _____, General Dyer ordered his soldiers to _____. More than 1,000 people were killed, and 1,000 were _____.

3 Gandhi was arrested and taken to _____. The _____ sent him to prison for six years. But two years later, Gandhi became very ill and he was _____.

Read Chapter 8. Put these events in the right order.

1 Thousands of people marched to the salt works at Dharasana.
2 Gandhi picked up a handful of salt from the sea.
3 Gandhi said that he was going to fight the salt tax.
4 The Viceroy said that people could collect salt from the sea.
5 Gandhi was arrested.
6 Gandhi and 78 other people began to march to Dandi.

Read Chapter 9. Are these sentences true (T) or false (F)?

1 Gandhi wanted Untouchables to have their own Assembly.
2 Gandhi called the Untouchables 'children of the mountains'.
3 In Poona, a bomb was thrown at Gandhi's car.
4 Jinnah wanted a separate nation for Muslims.
5 Gandhi thought that Germans should obey Hitler.
6 Gandhi ate little.

Read Chapters 10 and 11. Complete the sentences with the correct names.

Birla / Gandhi / Hitler / Kasturba / Nehru

1 In 1941, America joined the war against ______.
2 ______ died in Gandhi's arms.
3 ______ was a rich factory owner who often gave money to Gandhi's ashrams.
4 ______ travelled third-class by train to meet the Viceroy.
5 ______ became head of the new Indian government.

Read Chapters 12 and 13. Circle *a*, *b* or *c*.

1 When India was divided, a new nation called ______ was made.
a) Bengal b) Pakistan c) Punjab
2 After Gandhi had ______ for three days, the violence in Calcutta ended.
a) talked b) slept c) fasted
3 A bomb was thrown towards Gandhi when he was speaking at ______.
a) Congress b) a prayer meeting c) a wedding
4 Every day, Gandhi spent some time ______.
a) swimming b) running c) spinning
5 Gandhi was killed by a young ______ man.
a) Hindu b) Untouchable c) Muslim
6 Gandhi's last words were 'Oh ______'.
a) Mother b) God c) India
7 After Gandhi's death, Nehru said, 'The ______ has gone out of our lives'.
a) light b) happiness c) fire

ACTIVITIES

After Reading

1 **These two paragraphs are about Gandhi's life in two different places. Complete them using the words below.**

Africa, died, dreamed, Durban, England, English, experiences, first, guards, happy, head, Indian, judge, King, law, leaders, needed, oldest, refused, sad, three, turban, voyage, western

GANDHI IN ______

As a child, Mohandas ______ about going to London to study ______. Laxmidas, his ______ brother, paid for his journey. Mohandas bought a ticket and ______ clothes. The ______ took three weeks. On the ship, he ______ to eat meat. Mohandas finished his studies after ______ years. When he returned to India, he was ______ to hear that his mother had ______. Later in his life, Mohandas went back to the country and met many important ______, including ______ George the Fifth.

GANDHI IN SOUTH ______

Abdullah Sheth was the ______ of a law office in ______. He could not speak ______, and he ______ someone to help him work with his company's lawyers. Gandhi was ______ to go, because he wanted to have new ______. However, life was difficult for ______ people there. Once, a ______ told him to take off his ______ in court. Another time, the ______ on a train told Gandhi to move out of a ______ class compartment because a white person wanted to use it.

2 There are 18 words (4 letters or longer) from the book in this word search. Find the words (they go from left to right, and from top to bottom), and draw lines through them.

S	T	I	N	J	U	S	T	I	C	E	H	E	L
T	A	I	U	S	P	I	N	G	H	I	N	D	U
R	F	H	R	L	A	W	Y	E	R	T	H	I	V
I	R	E	S	A	S	G	P	R	I	S	O	N	I
K	I	M	E	M	A	R	C	H	S	O	N	D	O
E	K	P	G	U	J	A	R	A	T	I	E	I	L
O	A	I	U	T	M	U	S	L	I	M	O	G	E
F	A	R	M	E	R	F	O	U	A	R	L	O	N
I	N	E	A	M	B	U	L	A	N	C	E	V	C
E	S	V	E	G	E	T	A	R	I	A	N	S	E

1 Which three words are connected with religion?
2 Which three words are types of job?
3 Which two words are names of languages?

Write down all the letters that do not have lines through them. Begin with the first line, and go across each line to the end. There are 28 letters, making a sentence of 8 words.

4 What is the sentence?
5 Who said it?
6 What had just happened?

3 Perhaps this is what some of the people in this book are thinking. Who are they, and what are they thinking about?

1 'At last, we're coming home! We've been away for years. Look at all these people waiting for our ship! Of course, my husband is famous now, and the Indian people love him.'

2 'I've helped him here in South Africa. I've even been to prison. Now he lets my cousin study abroad, but he won't let me go. It's not fair! He went there when he was younger!'

3 'This is dangerous. There are thousands of Indians here, and they want to make trouble. I've told them that meetings are not allowed. My soldiers will have to stop them!'

4 'This man is very unusual. He is a peaceful man, and he has always spoken against violence. But he has been causing trouble for us, and the law says I must send him to prison.'

4 Do you agree or disagree with these sentences? Why?

1 People should always obey the law.

2 It is better for people with different religions to live separately.

3 Sometimes it is necessary for a person or a country to use violence.

4 Everyone should try to live a simple life like Gandhi's.

5 Compare Gandhi with another person that you admire (for example, a political leader or celebrity). How are they different, and how are they similar? Make a chart with information about them.

ABOUT THE AUTHOR

Rowena Akinyemi is British, and after many years in Africa, she now lives and works in Cambridge, though she still goes to Africa every year on holiday. She has worked in English Language Teaching for twenty-five years, in Africa and Britain, and has been writing ELT fiction for fifteen years. She has written several other stories for the Oxford Bookworms Library, including *Rainforests* and *Nelson Mandela* (Factfiles), and *Love or Money?* (Crime and Mystery). She has also adapted several stories for the same series, and her adaptation of *Cry Freedom* was a finalist in the Language Learner Literature Award, an international award for ELT readers, in 2004. She has also written books for children.

She has four children and is a keen football fan, supporting Manchester United. She enjoys country holidays in Britain – a long walk over hills or along cliffs in Wales, followed by a cream tea in a village teashop. But she also enjoys days in London shopping, walking on Hampstead Heath, looking at historical buildings, going to a concert or the theatre. She likes all sorts of music, especially African music, jazz, classical music, and Bob Dylan, and enjoys reading crime fiction and biographies.

When she was working on *Nelson Mandela* (Factfiles), Rowena became interested in the influence of Gandhi on the freedom struggle in South Africa. Her father was a pacifist, and she grew up with an admiration for the heroes of non-violence. Her family lived in Lancashire for ten years, near the town which Gandhi visited in 1931, when he travelled from London to meet Lancashire cotton workers.

OXFORD BOOKWORMS LIBRARY

Classics • Crime & Mystery • Factfiles • Fantasy & Horror
Human Interest • Playscripts • Thriller & Adventure
True Stories • World Stories

The OXFORD BOOKWORMS LIBRARY provides enjoyable reading in English, with a wide range of classic and modern fiction, non-fiction, and plays. It includes original and adapted texts in seven carefully graded language stages, which take learners from beginner to advanced level. An overview is given on the next pages.

All Stage 1 titles are available as audio recordings, as well as over eighty other titles from Starter to Stage 6. All Starters and many titles at Stages 1 to 4 are specially recommended for younger learners. Every Bookworm is illustrated, and Starters and Factfiles have full-colour illustrations.

The OXFORD BOOKWORMS LIBRARY also offers extensive support. Each book contains an introduction to the story, notes about the author, a glossary, and activities. Additional resources include tests and worksheets, and answers for these and for the activities in the books. There is advice on running a class library, using audio recordings, and the many ways of using Oxford Bookworms in reading programmes. Resource materials are available on the website <www.oup.com/elt/gradedreaders>.

The *Oxford Bookworms Collection* is a series for advanced learners. It consists of volumes of short stories by well-known authors, both classic and modern. Texts are not abridged or adapted in any way, but carefully selected to be accessible to the advanced student.

You can find details and a full list of titles in the *Oxford Bookworms Library Catalogue* and *Oxford English Language Teaching Catalogues*, and on the website <www.oup.com/elt/gradedreaders>.

THE OXFORD BOOKWORMS LIBRARY GRADING AND SAMPLE EXTRACTS

STARTER • 250 HEADWORDS

present simple – present continuous – imperative –
can/cannot, must – *going to* (future) – simple gerunds …

Her phone is ringing – but where is it?

Sally gets out of bed and looks in her bag. No phone. She looks under the bed. No phone. Then she looks behind the door. There is her phone. Sally picks up her phone and answers it. ***Sally's Phone***

STAGE 1 • 400 HEADWORDS

… past simple – coordination with *and, but, or* –
subordination with *before, after, when, because, so* …

I knew him in Persia. He was a famous builder and I worked with him there. For a time I was his friend, but not for long. When he came to Paris, I came after him – I wanted to watch him. He was a very clever, very dangerous man. ***The Phantom of the Opera***

STAGE 2 • 700 HEADWORDS

… present perfect – *will* (future) – *(don't) have to, must not, could* –
comparison of adjectives – simple *if* clauses – past continuous –
tag questions – *ask/tell* + infinitive …

While I was writing these words in my diary, I decided what to do. I must try to escape. I shall try to get down the wall outside. The window is high above the ground, but I have to try. I shall take some of the gold with me – if I escape, perhaps it will be helpful later. ***Dracula***

STAGE 3 • 1000 HEADWORDS

... *should, may* – present perfect continuous – *used to* – past perfect – causative – relative clauses – indirect statements ...

Of course, it was most important that no one should see Colin, Mary, or Dickon entering the secret garden. So Colin gave orders to the gardeners that they must all keep away from that part of the garden in future. ***The Secret Garden***

STAGE 4 • 1400 HEADWORDS

... past perfect continuous – passive (simple forms) – *would* conditional clauses – indirect questions – relatives with *where/when* – gerunds after prepositions/phrases ...

I was glad. Now Hyde could not show his face to the world again. If he did, every honest man in London would be proud to report him to the police. ***Dr Jekyll and Mr Hyde***

STAGE 5 • 1800 HEADWORDS

... future continuous – future perfect – passive (modals, continuous forms) – *would have* conditional clauses – modals + perfect infinitive ...

If he had spoken Estella's name, I would have hit him. I was so angry with him, and so depressed about my future, that I could not eat the breakfast. Instead I went straight to the old house. ***Great Expectations***

STAGE 6 • 2500 HEADWORDS

... passive (infinitives, gerunds) – advanced modal meanings – clauses of concession, condition

When I stepped up to the piano, I was confident. It was as if I knew that the prodigy side of me really did exist. And when I started to play, I was so caught up in how lovely I looked that I didn't worry how I would sound. ***The Joy Luck Club***

BOOKWORMS · FACTFILES · STAGE 3

Martin Luther King

ALAN C. McLEAN

The United States in the 1950s and 60s was a troubled place. Black people were angry, because they did not have the same rights as whites. It was a time of angry words, of marches, of protests, a time of bombs and killings.

But above the angry noise came the voice of one man – a man of peace. 'I have a dream,' said Martin Luther King, and it was a dream of blacks and whites living together in peace and freedom. This is the story of an extraordinary man, who changed American history in his short life.

BOOKWORMS · FACTFILES · STAGE 4

Nelson Mandela

ROWENA AKINYEMI

In 1918 in the peaceful province of Transkei, South Africa, the Mandela family gave their new baby son the name Rolihlahla – 'troublemaker'. But the young boy's early years were happy ones, and he grew up to be a good student and an enthusiastic sportsman.

Who could imagine then what was waiting for Nelson Mandela – the tireless struggle for human rights, the long years in prison, the happiness and sadness of family life, and one day the title of President of South Africa? This is the story of an extraordinary man, recognized today as one of the world's great leaders, whose long walk to freedom brought new hope to a troubled nation.